28-Day CBT Workbook For Adults

Start Rewiring Your Brain In:

15 Minutes a Day

With Proven Techniques For Anxiety, Stress, & Self-Esteem

Calvin Caufield

Table of Contents

Introduction

When Sarah entered my office, she appeared to be shaking like a leaf. She had suffered from anxiety all her life. During my sessions with her, I would realize that meeting new people was anxiety-provoking for her. It took her immense courage to show up to my office that day. Fifteen minutes into the session, Sarah had calmed down enough for us to discuss her goals from therapy.

I realized quickly Sarah found it hard to relax. Her mind had a special talent for thinking of the worst possible scenario, no matter what the situation. This anxiety made it difficult for her to progress in her career. She knew she was capable of being a manager but whenever it came to giving presentations or talking to higher-ups in the team, she found herself stuttering, and her mind went blank. Oftentimes, she had to rush to the washroom to calm herself down. Occasionally, she found herself close to tears. She used to get frustrated and hopeless that she would never be successful in her career.

It was her frustration that finally led her to giving CBT a try. She had a presentation in 10 days and wanted to work on her anxiety related to it. Knowing well that 10 days was a short time to work on her thoughts, which were the main cause of her anxiety, I focused on giving her tools to manage her anxiety. In our session after her presentation, Sarah told me she still had very high anxiety and all the physical and behavioral symptoms were there but because of the tools she now had from our time together, she was able to mask it well and not let it affect her performance. Over the next few weeks, we picked apart Sarah's thinking patterns and worked on challenging her dysfunctional thoughts which were causing her anxiety in the first place.

Sixteen sessions later, Sarah smiled as she thanked me for our work together. Over the last 4 months, Sarah had learnt how to cope with her anxiety. She had even talked to her superior about being considered for a promotion. Not only did she give that presentation at her job, but she had made several presentations since we started working together and reported getting better with each one. She had managed to do a range of personal, professional, and social activities that she had never found the nerve for, earlier. It was an incredible transformation, but if you're familiar with CBT you'll know that it's not uncommon.

It all comes down to the power of our thoughts. Our thoughts, in many ways, are the lenses through which we view the world. If our thoughts are distorted and negative, then that shades our view of the world and ourselves.

Unfortunately, in our fast-paced world people have been experiencing higher rates of depression and anxiety[1]. This can be attributed to a variety of reasons including biological (chemical changes in the brain, hormones), psychological (personality, coping mechanisms), social (lack of social support), and economic (unemployment) among others. Depression and anxiety are disabling disorders that prevent you from reaching your fullest potential and having a good quality of life. Other negative feelings like anger, fear, and low self-esteem are also detrimental.

In my work with Sarah, I used techniques from Cognitive Behavior Therapy (CBT) to shift her out of these negative thoughts and feelings, and towards more empowering beliefs. But it's not just for people with anxiety. CBT is an evidence-based therapy that has been successful for treating:

- Depression and Dysthymia
- Bipolar Disorder
- Anxiety Disorders
- Somatoform Disorders
- Eating Disorders
- Insomnia
- Personality Disorders
- Anger and Aggression
- Substance Use
- Schizophrenia
- General Stress
- Distress Due to General Medical Conditions
- Chronic Pain and Fatigue
- Distress related to Pregnancy Complications and Female Hormonal Conditions[2]

CBT is a commonly used approach by therapists worldwide when working with clients with depression, anxiety, and fear states among other disorders. CBT orients you to the power of thoughts. In everyday life, our thoughts govern both our feelings and our actions. Oftentimes, we misinterpret that a situation is what leads to our feelings, and subsequent behaviors. But in reality, it's not the situation but our interpretation of the situation, or in simple terms, our thoughts about the situation that determine our feelings and actions.

This book offers you an understanding of CBT and how to apply the principles in an easy-to-understand manner in your day-to-day life to be able to cope with feelings of sadness, anxiety, anger, fear and to improve your self-esteem. This book teaches you in a quick practical way how to start putting the most useful and proven parts of CBT to work right away.

As a coach, I have used CBT with my clients, with techniques right from the days of my training. I have seen what changes it has made in the life of my clients, and I want you to get those benefits too. I understand how difficult it might seem to be able to overcome issues of anxiety and depression. I am aware of how these mood states affect not only your personal life but also your professional and social life. These states make it harder for you to be what you are capable of, and cause a huge amount of distress and disruption.

One of my favorite things about working with clients using CBT is the range of 'aha moments' I get to witness when clients discover so much about themselves in the process. It's heartening to see, every single time! I have seen clients blossom week after week of using CBT and the change in their mood presents a reliable measure of their progress. This is why I am really eager to show you how using the right tools can make a tremendous difference to your quality of life.

Whether you're reading this book by yourself or you're using it in conjunction with your therapy or coaching, you are bound to see the benefits it will bring to your life. I understand not everyone has the time or resources to go into therapy or coaching. That is exactly why I wrote this book. I want more and more people to be able to live their fullest lives. CBT has been proven effective for over 6 decades now. There's science behind it. My agenda in writing this book is to simplify and break down the principles of CBT where they are easily understandable and applicable by readers.

How to Use This Workbook

Whenever we want to change something about our life – a habit, a routine, a way of doing things, the first step is commitment. Each day has activities and core ideas of CBT broken down for you to read through and complete in 15 minutes a day. However, always feel free to go at your own pace. Some activities may help clarify something you're already fairly aware of and go more quickly for you. While others may address something you haven't considered before. If you truly only have 15 minutes or struggle with motivation, then by all means feel free to do even just one activity per day, and return to the next activity in that chapter the following day. There's value to each activity so you'll progress even going at a slower pace. Everyone's journey is different and there is no rush. Take as little or as much time as you need. This is something that is important to you and that's why you bought this workbook. I want you to be able to make the most of it.

You don't go to the gym for a day and expect results, right? The same is true for your mind. I need you to be consistent with the process. If you stay consistent for 4 weeks, I promise not only you but people close to you will notice the difference it brings to your life. For your ease, I have broken down this workbook into 28 days so that you know when to stop for each day.

This 28-day workbook is designed such that each day builds on the previous one. The workbook is divided into several parts to make the process easy to follow and less overwhelming. The days are organized sequentially, starting with defining your goals and values to establish clarity on what is most meaningful to you to work on. After you have your goals to work on, the second step is to identify the obstacles in your roadmap. More often than not, these hurdles are usually your own negative thoughts. So, in part 2 of the workbook, you will pay close attention to your thoughts and begin to identify common errors in thinking that you may be making. These thoughts lay the groundwork for negative emotional reactions like anxiety or sadness, and impact your behaviors in an adverse manner.

In part 3 of the workbook, you will be engaging in action-based strategies to test out your thinking errors and to engage in pleasurable activities. This would ensure that the change is not merely in your thoughts but translates to actions in your daily life. The timing of each activity is intentional, ensuring you are ready to take them on, when they appear in the workbook. A mid-program check-in is placed on Day 15 to ensure you are reflecting your progress, celebrating your achievements, and adjusting your goals to remain in sync with your requirements.

Part 4 is targeted towards managing your anxieties and fears. You will understand in depth what is happening in your mind and body when you face these emotions. You will then learn techniques to lower your fears and anxiety. During this time of the workbook, you will learn to bring together all elements of CBT: your thoughts, physical symptoms, and behaviors, in order to work on your fears and anxieties. You will be learning ways to face your anxieties and fears instead of avoiding them.

In part 5 of the workbook, you will work on your deep-rooted and resistant-to-change beliefs which maintain your anxiety, stress, and low self-esteem among other negative impacts. You will deep dive to understand their origin before challenging and reframing them. You will learn to foster a positive mindset to ensure your continued growth and build emotional resilience. At the end of week 3, you will do a self-check-in to track your progress, adjust your goals, and highlight learnings to carry along with you.

Part 6 of the workbook works specifically on dealing with anger and feelings of sadness. You will learn what purpose anger serves in your life and to be able to find ways to constructively express anger. You will learn techniques to manage your anger via your thoughts, physical responses, and behaviors. To manage depressive symptoms, you will collate your learning from previous days and apply it accordingly. You will also learn to act in an adaptive manner to find social support and talk to yourself in a compassionate manner.

The final part of this workbook focuses on building self-esteem and inculcating self-acceptance. You will identify other practical uses for the techniques you have been learning to positively impact other domains of your life. The last day is planned to help you integrate your learning from the workbook and make a daily plan to continue to practice what you have learnt.

As you begin your journey through this workbook, make sure to be consistent and patient. Each small step will help you get closer to your goals. By the end of this workbook, you will emerge with a better understanding of yourself and will be better equipped to deal with the struggles you encounter in your life. All I ask is for you to stay committed, and trust in this process of growth and change. Let's do this!

PART 1

Defining your Goals and Values

During the first 4 days in this 28-day CBT workbook, we will be focusing on setting your personal goals and identifying your values. It is very important to highlight what truly matters to you so that you are working towards bringing a meaningful change in your life. Whether you want to work on your low self-esteem, anxiety, or health goals, being aware of your personal values would be beneficial to lead you to living a purposeful life.

The first step of CBT is to identify your personal concerns so that you can make the most of this workbook by achieving your goals as you reach Day 28. Once you have specific goals in mind, you would be able to become aware of your thoughts, feelings, and behaviors which are becoming obstacles in your path to reach your desired goals. For example, if you have low self-esteem, perhaps the obstacle is your thoughts about yourself and the negative self-talk you indulge in. If you suffer from anxiety episodes, maybe you find it hard to relax and often find yourself overthinking.

By identifying your problem areas and then making goals around them, you are recognizing the cause of the problem and will eventually be working on alleviating it. The focus on values is to make sure your daily goals are aligning with your values so that you are able to work on them in the long-term. Once you are able to recognize what is most meaningful to you – freedom, relationships, professional accolades, for example – you will be able to make progress in that area by removing any hindrances. Our aim in the next 4 days is to make realistic daily goals based on your values in order to lay the groundwork for meaningful change in the upcoming days.

DAY 1:

Identifying What Really Matters

As we begin this journey together, it would be helpful to figure out which areas of your life could use some practical help. Are there any specific problems or areas of concern that you have been facing currently? Cognitive Behavior Therapy works best when you have clear concerns to work with.

When Kira–a former client of mine–came to me, she was struggling with a lot of things. She said, "My life is a mess. Nothing seems to be going right. No matter what I do or how hard I try, I can't seem to make anything okay." After I gave her space and time to air out her emotions, she was able to get into a comparatively calm state of mind. We started to make a list of all life areas and how she was doing on each of them to understand if any areas were working well, while pointing out real concerns that needed to be addressed.

Let's assess your concerns with a similar exercise.

ACTIVITY:
Life Domain Score

Think about the following areas of your life. Assign a satisfaction score to each of them from very dissatisfied (score of 1) to very satisfied (10).

Life Domain	Score
Self-Esteem	
Relationships	
Professional life	
Health	
Finances	
Living Situation	
Personal Development	
Hobbies	

Are there any areas with a score of 5 or less? These are worth making a note of as they may be resulting in negative emotions. Now for the low-scoring domains, elaborate on your current concerns in these life areas.

Example:
Relationships: I feel like I don't have anyone to talk to.
Professional Life: I feel burnt out. I am stressed and can't seem to relax even on weekends.

ACTIVITY:
Current Concerns

Elaborate on your concerns below

Life Domain:

_____

Current Concerns:

_____

_____

_____

Life Domain:

_____

Current Concerns:

_____

_____

_____

If you feel like you are facing issues in multiple domains, either stack your concerns by the lowest score or on the basis of priority what you would like to work on to begin with.

List of Current Concerns based on priority
1.
2.
3.

Once you know the priority of working with your concerns, let's understand the impact they have on your life.

How do these concerns affect your life? Reflect on what areas of your life are impacted by your current problems.

Example:
Work:
I feel burnt out. I am stressed and can't seem to relax even on weekends.
Areas affected:
Physical and mental health – I feel tired and stressed out.
Self-care – I can't find time to exercise or read a book.
Relationships – I am irritable and get angry quickly at my wife and kids.

ACTIVITY:
Understanding the Impact

Note the impact of your concern.

Concern:
Areas Impacted:

How are these concerns impacting the way you think, feel, or behave?

Example:
Being burnt out at work makes me think 'no matter how much I do, it never seems to be enough; my manager is not happy with me and if I don't work on weekends and accomplish this goal, he might kick me out.' It makes me feel 'not good enough', disheartened, tired, and frustrated. I end up taking out my anger on my family, I am hardly getting any sleep because of the constant worry, and I don't take out time to have a proper meal.

Now think about how your concerns are impacting your thoughts, feelings, and behavior.

Concern

_____

_____

_____

_____

Impact on Thoughts

_____

_____

Impact on Feelings

_____

_____

Impact on Behavior

_____

_____

In order to go further in-depth of these concerns, ask yourself why questions over and over again until you feel like you have reached the cause of the concern. Look at the example in the following image. The process led to the root cause of the problem being fear of rejection.

Concern
Relationships: I feel like I don't have anyone to talk to.

↓

Why
do I feel like I don't have anyone to talk to?

↓

Because
every time I want to talk to someone, I draw up a blank.

↓

Why
do I draw a blank?

↓

Because
I feel like everyone is busy and no one calls or starts talking to me.

↓

Why
am I not calling them or starting conversations with them?

↓

Because
Because I feel they might not pick up or respond and I'll feel rejected.

↓

Root Cause:
This process showed the root cause of the problem is fear of rejection.

ACTIVITY:

Getting to the Root Cause

Try it here with one of your concerns.

Concern

↓

Why

↓

Because

↓

Why

↓

Because

↓

Why

↓

Because

↓

Root Cause:

In order to address any concern, it is important to understand its root cause. Anxiety, stress, emotional eating, or relationship conflicts are all outward behaviors that are being caused by our root issues. If we only work on the surface symptoms, we will see a decline in concerned problems but only for a short period. If we want to dig out the problem from its root, we need to work on the cause. These causes could be trauma during childhood, negative thought patterns, or unaddressed emotions. Addressing the source of the concern would lead to a longer-lasting improvement than merely working on the symptoms. Through the use of CBT, our aim is to lead to a lasting and meaningful change.

Identifying the root cause helps you target the right problem and gives you insight into what needs to be worked upon. This self-awareness helps you focus on the true cause of the problem.

DAY 2:

Creating SMART Goals

You are now aware of your problem areas, their root causes and their impact on your thoughts, feelings, behaviors, and overall life. Before we start working on them, we need to make some goals. Goals are important not only to keep us on track but also to monitor progress. In CBT, setting goals is important to structure the process of change. When you have structured goals, you can break them down into manageable parts and avoid being overwhelmed. Goals ensure you remain motivated and have a direction to work towards. CBT requires that you have concrete goals like 'I want to exercise 3 days a week for 30 minutes each to work my fitness' instead of abstract goals like 'I want to get fit.'

Take the case of Gerald, for example. This former client of mine looked exuberant and full of energy when he told me he had so many goals and he knew exactly what he wanted. He said he didn't need my help in making goals, he needed my help to reach them. He just couldn't understand that despite having this zeal and energy, why he was not able to reach his goals. When I looked at his goals list, I could see how organized and methodical he was. He had goals for each area of his life. He had daily, weekly, monthly, and yearly goals. He knew exactly what he wanted. But he was still not getting there. In order to understand what was going wrong, let me tell you more about goals and the process of setting them.

Goals should be:

Specific: Keep it as clear and specific as possible.

Measurable: In order to monitor progress, we should be able to measure it.

Achievable: It should be a realistic goal. Setting too far-fetched a goal will only result in demotivation and frustration.

Relevant: It should be a goal relevant to your overall life objectives.

Time-bound: The goals should have a deadline.

Based on your concern list from the previous day, let us make some SMART goals. Let's look at an example from Day 1.

- **Life Domain:** Relationships
- **Current Concern:** I feel like I don't have anyone to talk to.
- **Areas Impacted:** Personal well-being
- **Root Cause:** Fear of Rejection

Based on this information, your goal would require you to do something on the social front. "I feel like I don't have anyone to talk to but based on identifying my root cause, I realized that is not true. It is my fear of rejection which is making me feel like this. In order to work on my relationships domain, I need to be in touch with my friends, which is my goal."

Note: 'Fear of rejection' is a deep-rooted cause which would require more work on the thoughts. This would be worked upon on Day 19. For the present scenario, focus more on action-oriented goals and not those which require changing a deep-rooted thought pattern.

Specific: Define your goal in detail. What exactly do you want to achieve? Ask yourself these questions to make sure it is a specific goal.

- What do I want to achieve?
- Why do I want to achieve it?
- Is there any other person involved in my reaching this goal?
- What resources are available to me?
- What are the barriers I am facing?

Example Goal: I want to be in touch with my friends.

I want to do it so that I have someone to reach out to and depend on when needed. I would require the cooperation of my friends to achieve this goal. I have a few close friends. I can get in touch with them over text, call, email, or in person. I am facing the barrier of my own fear of rejection.

Measurable: How will you measure if you are succeeding at your goal? What would indicate progress on the goal? I will measure my progress based on how frequently I am in touch with my friends.

Achievable: Is it an achievable goal at the moment? Do I have enough resources? Yes, I have enough resources and different modes to be in touch with my friends.

Relevant: Why is this goal important for me? Does it align with my life goals? Is it the right time for me to work on this goal? I value social support. It is an important coping mechanism for me. I value friendships and friends have always been an important part of my life. It is important for me to work on this goal right now because if I don't, I will keep distancing myself from my friends and eventually lose them.

Time-bound: When do I want to achieve this? What can I do tomorrow? Next week? Next month? In 3 months? I will get in touch with 3 of my closest friends in the next 2 weeks. I will text/ call/ meet them.

Going back to Gerald, his goals were relevant and important to him. He was doing good on that aspect, the others not so much. His goals were too general (not specific; I want to be physically fit). Even though he would keep a measure (body weight), his goals were not achievable (I want to lose 7 pounds each week). He set himself unrealistic goals and thus, unconsciously, set himself up for failure. When we made SMART goals in the session together, Gerald slowly (too slow for his liking) but gradually began to achieve his goals. Over time, he realized that he was setting unrealistic goals and as much as he wanted to achieve them quickly, it was not feasible to do so.

ACTIVITY:
Making SMART Goals

Area of Concern:
Goal:
Specific:
Measurable:
Achievable:
Relevant:
Time-Bound:

You have made 1 SMART goal that is important and relevant to you at this moment. You're encouraged to make a few more, or just stick to one for now. For the next 3 weeks, we will be working on these goals. You may achieve some goals quickly, while others may require more effort and time.

The key is to be able to evaluate if and when a goal needs to be tweaked. Be mindful of tracking your progress. This will help you understand once you have reached a goal and can focus on the others. Also, sometimes our goals change so you would need to be more open and accepting of that. Over the next few weeks, tweak, add, or let go of a goal, depending on its relevance in your life currently.

DAY 3:

Clarifying Your Core Values

Core values are the sets of beliefs you have developed and acquired over your lifespan. They guide your behaviors in your day-to-day life and help you make the right decisions for yourself. The focus of CBT is to make purposeful change for the better. When your core values are aligned with your day-to-day goals, you are looking at making longer-term lasting change, which is the aim of CBT. You made some goals yesterday. It is important to align them with your personal values to give them a sense of purpose, ensuring your consistent motivation to achieve them.

Ben was always curious about things. As a child, he used to ask a million questions to his exasperated parents. Even as an adult, that quality stayed with him. It was important for him to learn new information and skills. He valued lifelong learning. He felt a sense of wonder and had an eagerness to discover new things, places, and people.

Let's begin by trying to identify your personal values. Some examples would be honesty (being truthful in all situations is important to me), relationships (spending time with loved ones is my priority), growth (I don't want to be static, I want to continue learning and growing), health (being fit, mentally or physically, holds importance for me), freedom (I want to be free to do what I want, when I want to).

ACTIVITY:
Identifying Your Core Values

1.	
2.	
3.	
4.	
5.	
6.	
7.	
8.	
9.	
10.	

Pick the top 3 based on your priorities. Which 3 are the most important for you? Asking yourself the following questions will help you to make the choice:

- In adverse circumstances, which values have helped me the most?

- Which values show up in my daily actions?

- Even when no one is watching, which values do I continue to reflect?

ACTIVITY:
Identify Your Top Priorities

1.
2.
3.

Now let's delve a bit deeper into these values.

- Do you remember the origin of this value?

- Why is it so important for you?

- How does it contribute to your life?

Example: **Financial Independence.**
Do you remember the origin of this value?
Growing up, Gina always saw how much her mom struggled with not having her own finances. She always felt stuck and had nowhere to go even when she had major conflicts with Gina's father. Gina remembers feeling she never wants to be in that position.

Why is it so important for you??
She said, "I need to be able to feel free about spending whenever and wherever I want to. I do not want to have to ask someone for money to fulfill my needs and wishes."

How does it contribute to your life?
"Relationships may come and go but always having the resources to look after myself will ensure my quality of life. Financial independence adds to my sense of self-worth and self-esteem. I am confident in my abilities," Gina said.

ACTIVITY:
Your Primary Values

Core Value:

Do you remember the origin of this value?

Why is it so important for you?

How does it contribute to your life?

Core Value:

Do you remember the origin of this value?

Why is it so important for you?

How does it contribute to your life?

Core Value:
Do you remember the origin of this value?
Why is it so important for you?
How does it contribute to your life?

Once you have clarity of your core values, let us align them with your goals. Referring to yesterday's exercise, check if the goals you made align with your values. If not, how can you adjust them to bring them closer to your values? Ask yourself the following questions:

- Does this goal align with my values?

- How will achieving this goal ensure I am living by my values?

- What can I do to align this goal with my values?

Example:
Goal: I want to be in touch with my friends.
Aligned Value: Relationships (this goal will deepen my friendships).

What are some daily action plans based on your core values and goals?

Example:
Goal: I want to be in touch with my friends.
Aligned Value: Relationships
Action Plan: Text one friend daily

Example:
Goal: I want to be healthy.
Aligned Value: Fitness
Daily Action Plan: Do 30 mins exercise.

ACTIVITY:
Align Your Goals & Values

Goal	Aligned Value	Daily Action Plan

DAY 4:

Mapping Your Goals

The action-oriented approach of CBT requires not only to identify relevant problems but also to make actionable plans to bring about changes in behavior. When we map our goals, we break them down into realistic, actionable items while identifying any possible obstacles.

Walter, a former client, always had umpteen number of things he wanted to do with his time. He wanted to play golf, learn to play the guitar, meditate daily, and learn to cook Thai food among other things. He even attempted some of these. But after a week or two of lessons, he always found himself demotivated or short of time. He felt like he didn't have enough time in the day. He was very meticulous and would schedule everything on his calendar. Early morning meditation followed by 1 hour guitar lesson, and a golf lesson in the evening after which he would try to cook Thai from a YouTube video. After 5 days of following the schedule, he just wanted to watch his favorite TV series instead of playing golf and making dinner. So, he would put everything off his list for another time and so on.

Can you relate with Walter? You make goals, maybe act on them for a day or two, a week and then it gets harder and harder to continue them, so you give up. Amidst other reasons for this, a major one is trying to do too much all at once. If you don't exercise at all and your goal is to exercise for an hour, and you start doing it from Day 1, chances are you will be back to no exercise by Day 8. Goal mapping is about breaking down big goals into small, achievable ones to ensure not only do you accomplish them but also sustain them for the longer term.

ACTIVITY:
Identify Milestones

Example:
Goal: Exercise daily
Milestones:

1. Decide on the type of exercise.

2. Identify a place (space in home/ gym/ dance class)

3. Schedule a time

4. Exercise 2-3 times per week

Look at the table and write your goal at the top. Then fill out the milestones labeled milestone 1, milestone 2, milestone 3, and milestone 4. You'll be filling out the rest of the table in the next activities.

Goal:_____

_____

Milestone 1: _____

Step 1: _____	Step 2: _____	Step 3:_____
_____	_____	_____
_____	_____	_____
_____	_____	_____
Done by:_____	Done by:_____	Done by:_____

Milestone 2:_____

Step 1: _____	Step 2: _____	Step 3:_____
_____	_____	_____
_____	_____	_____
_____	_____	_____
Done by:_____	Done by:_____	Done by:_____

Goal:_____

_____

Milestone 3:_____

Step 1: _____	Step 2: _____	Step 3: _____
_____	_____	_____
_____	_____	_____
_____	_____	_____
Done by:_____	Done by:_____	Done by: _____

Milestone 4:_____

Step 1: _____	Step 2: _____	Step 3: _____
_____	_____	_____
_____	_____	_____
_____	_____	_____
Done by:_____	Done by:_____	Done by: _____

These milestones can be further broken down into smaller action points.

Example: Decide on the type of exercise.

- Identify all my available options.
- Try a few things to see what I like the best.
- Hire an instructor/ get a gym membership/ join a class.

ACTIVITY:
Break Down Your Milestones

Go back to the table in the previous page and write down the smaller steps for your milestones.
Make sure to prioritize and schedule these steps in the logical order before carrying them out.

Example:
Goal: Exercise Daily
Milestones:

- Decide on the type of exercise Step 1: Identify all my available options
- Step 2: Try few things to see what I like the best
- Step 3: Hire an instructor/ get a gym membership/ join a class

ACTIVITY:
Milestone Timelines

Now that you know what needs to be done, you need to set a deadline for each milestone and action point so that you don't end up procrastinating it. Make sure the deadline is realistic but also not too far into the future. Find the right balance. Go back to the table in the previous page and write down your milestone timelines.

Example:

Goal: Exercise Daily

Milestones:

- Decide on the type of exercise – 4 weeks

- Step 1: Identify all my available options – done by: Week 1

- Step 2: Try few things to see what I like the best – done by: Week 2-3

- Step 3: Hire an instructor/ get a gym membership/ join a class – done by Week 4

If you'd like to reuse this goal setting template in the future, you can do so by accessing the pdf available via the QR code, or by using this link: *https:// bit.ly/28-cbt*

It seems like we have got everything covered and you must be getting ready to put this plan into action but we're not completely there yet. Look back at how many weeks, months, or years you have wanted to work on some of these goals. Or perhaps think about how many times you have started but not stayed consistent with your goals. It would help you understand that achieving a goal is not just about starting right but also about being able to maintain consistency. There is a reason why it has taken you so long to get started/ stick with your goals. Let's identify some of the challenges and obstacles you have faced. What gets in your way of starting/ maintaining this goal?

Example:

Goal: Exercise Regularly

Challenge: Lack of time or motivation

We are trying to prevent these challenges from keeping you away from achieving your goal. This requires not only to identify obstacles but also to propose relevant solutions to overcoming them.

Challenge: Lack of time
Proposed Solution: Schedule time in calendar based on feasibility/ find time on weekends
Challenge: Lack of motivation
Proposed Solution: Find a gym partner/ someone to keep me accountable

ACTIVITY:
Identify Obstacle & Solutions

Goal	Challenge	Proposed Solution

Over the last 4 days you have identified your areas of concern, made SMART goals, defined your personal values, and mapped your goals. Now that you know what you want to accomplish through this workbook, tomorrow you will learn more about Cognitive Behavior Therapy and how it can help you accomplish your goals.

PART 2

Identifying and Challenging Negative Thoughts

Now that you have identified your goals and values, it is important to explore one of the major obstacles which keep you from achieving your goals – your negative thoughts. Negative thoughts make you doubt your capabilities, make you fearful and hesitant in working towards your goals. Thus, in the next 4 days, you will be learning about negative thought patterns so that you can identify your patterns that make it hard for you to reach your goals. Once you realize what these roadblocks are, you can challenge and remove them from your path to goal achievement.

These patterns, known as cognitive distortions or errors in thinking are faulty ways of thinking that lead to depression, anxiety, and low self-esteem among other dysfunctional consequences. This kind of thinking results in negative emotional reactions and maladaptive behaviors. CBT helps us to identify these errors in our thinking and to challenge these thoughts.

Common cognitive distortions include black-and-white thinking where you might view situations or people as either all good or all bad, overgeneralization (generalizing from a single event), and labeling (making a judgment about self or others). These distortions affect how you think about yourself, others, or the world in general. They contribute to low self-esteem, anxiety reactions, or hopelessness, and create hurdles in completing daily activities of life.

As you start to become aware of your cognitive distortions, you are able to question their reality. The goal of the next 4 days is to understand cognitive distortions, recognize how they play out in your thinking, and to begin to challenge them. For example, instead of thinking, 'I am stupid' (labeling, overgeneralization), you might think, 'I made a mistake, but I can be more careful in the future.' By changing the way you think, this workbook aims at changing the way you feel and behave and minimizes negative emotional reactions.

Breaking Down How Your Mind Works

Alex, a 30-year-old accountant, was working at his desk when his manager called him over the phone and said that he needed to see Alex immediately. As soon as Alex disconnected the call, his mind went through a million different scenarios of why the manager wanted to see him on an urgent basis. Was it about the vacation time he had recently taken, or the oversight on the last project, or perhaps that he had come 10 minutes late to the office today? His heartbeat rising, Alex got up from his desk and was sweating profusely by the time he reached the manager's office. He stuttered as he made the manager aware of his presence, "Yes, Sir?"

Nadine, a 35-year-old customer service executive was jotting down details of her latest call when the manager intimated to her over the phone that she needed to see her urgently. Nadine got up from her desk, and while taking a quick sip of water, wondered what this could be about. Her mind raced back to how many calls she had turned to sales recently, and she imagined perhaps there was a compliment, reward, or even a promotion coming her way. As she walked to the manager's office, her head held high, she was smiling when she checked with the manager if she could come in.

Did you notice how the situation in the examples above was similar but the behavior of the two individuals was starkly different from each other? Even their physical reactions were in contrast to each other. What do you think affected how they reacted to and behaved in the situation?

If you guessed it was what they thought at that moment, you would be right. And that is the power of thoughts. In our day-to-day life, thoughts affect both our feelings and our actions. We often misinterpret that a situation is what leads to our feelings, and subsequent behaviors. But it is our thoughts about the situation that impact our feelings and actions.[3]

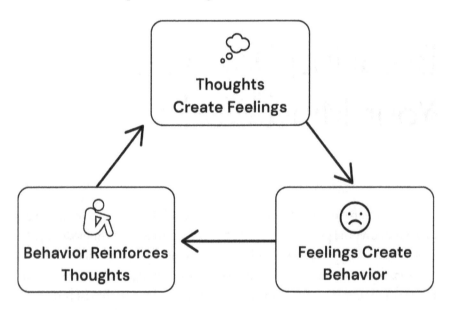

How else would you explain why different people react in a different manner to a similar situation? This contrast is starker in highly intense circumstances, when we find ourselves in a situation which we believe is dangerous. Let's take the example of Philip who is walking in a park and sees a large dog off leash running towards him. His heart in his throat, he runs in the opposite direction as fast as he can and doesn't stop until he reaches his home and decides never to go to that park again.

On the other hand, Kent, when faced with a large dog off his leash running towards him, gets worried. He looks around and calmly calls for a possible owner, while getting out of the dog's way, only to realize that the dog was running after a thrown ball. He notices the owner who is now in sight and laughs-off his reaction while continuing his walk.

The situation above could be potentially dangerous and thus, the feelings Philip and Kent felt were similar, but their intensity of the feeling was different. And based on their thoughts during the situation, not only was their immediate behavior different but it also affected their longer-term behavior. While Philip decided he didn't want to go to that park ever again, Kent would continue to visit there. Another possible long-term impact of this situation on Philip could be his fear of large dogs causing another similar circumstance in the future and this fear might become disabling in his day-to-day functioning.

Now that you have some idea of how important a function thoughts play in determining our feelings and behaviors, let me show you how we can use this understanding to alleviate some of the negative feelings we experience in our day-to-day lives. The first step would be to monitor how this plays out in your life. Are you aware of your frequent thoughts? Did you know we have anywhere between 12000 to 60000 thoughts per day[4]? That's a lot of thoughts to keep account of. So how about this? What if you jotted down some of your daily thoughts in intense situations to understand how your mind works? Think of your mind as a machine. You can't fix a machine if you don't know anything about it. Let's get to know your mind better.

ACTIVITY:
Thought-Feeling-Behavior

An hour or so before bed, take out 10 minutes to think back on your day. Identify 1-3 situations that you had intense reactions to. Think of situations in which you felt anxious, sad, angry, frustrated, or any other similar feeling. Filling out the below template would give you an insight into how your brain works on a typical day. We need as many of these situations and their details as you can remember. This exercise is to be continued for the next few days in order to get a good sample to make some conclusions from. Here's an example to get you started.

Date: _June 16, 2024_

Situation: I was running 10mins late to pick up my son from school as my meeting went on longer than expected.

Thought(s):

My son would be so upset. His teachers would think less of me. I am such an incompetent father.

Behavior:

I drove faster than normal to get there as soon as possible. I avoided eye contact with the teachers while apologizing, thanking them profusely.

Feeling(s):

Guilt

Frustration

The situation above is quite a common one and it happens to the best of us. We get late sometimes and feel guilty and/ or frustrated about it. I hope this gives you an idea of a simple situation from your day that you can note down here. So put that daily reminder in your phone and make sure you jot down some incidents at the end of your day.

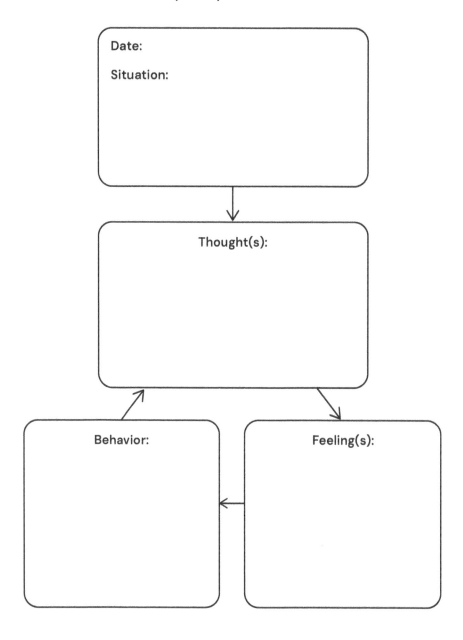

DAY 6:

Recognizing Faulty Thinking Patterns

Remember I told you how many thoughts we get every day? There is a wide variety to them. They can be positive or negative in nature. They can be a one-time or a frequently repetitive thought. And they can be rational or not. Sometimes we are able to identify when a thought seems irrational or illogical but quite often, we do not recognize it. We make errors in our thinking. Since we do not realize we are making an error, we end up repeating it, over and over again. Thoughts, unlike behaviors, are internal, so most well-wishers are unable to point out the irrationality of our thoughts.

Negative automatic thoughts are thoughts that come to our mind instantly and are hard to push away. They are automatic and hence go by unnoticed. They significantly impact our feelings and consequent behaviors. It is, thus, important to be aware of our negative automatic thoughts and engage in self-monitoring. Peter has been wanting to get into a certain prestigious university for his further studies. He has spent days and nights working on his applications. Despite all his efforts, he did not manage to secure admission. Brokenhearted, he decides to try again next year. Unfortunately, he still didn't get in. He refuses to even apply to other universities. So, he has decided to attempt again for the third year.

When we look at his first attempt, we are able to see how hardworking and determined Peter is to achieve his goals. It is a positive feature of his personality.

But when we look at his ongoing behavior, we realize he's engaging in what is a cognitive error called black-and-white thinking or all or none error. He needs to get into this university at all costs. If he is unable to do that, he feels like a complete failure and sees nothing more to life.

Cognitive distortions are irrational ways of thinking that impact our feelings and subsequent behaviors. Like Peter, it is often difficult to recognize the error when you are the one making it. Peter believes he is just going after his goal and there is nothing wrong with working towards a dream. So, he is unable to notice when a great goal changes into something that is actually stopping him from living up to his full potential.

Let me introduce you to other common cognitive distortions.

- **Catastrophizing/ Magnification.** Thinking of the worst possible outcome.
  Example: "I am going to embarrass myself during the presentation."

- **Overgeneralization.** Generalizing something based on a single event.
  Example: "Walt thinks to himself, 'She never comes on time,' when his girlfriend is late for a lunch date, even though she is rarely late."

- **Jumping to conclusions.** Assuming you know the other person's thoughts or can predict the future.
  Example: "She didn't even look at me today, I am sure she is mad at me for something."

- **Mental filtering.** Focusing on the negative while excluding the positive.
  Example: "I got 45/50 on my assignment the other day. I am so disappointed in myself for losing out on those 5 marks."

- **Discounting the positive.** Disregarding positive attributes or behaviors as being insignificant or not important enough.
  Example: "Oh, I am sure, anyone could have done it. It was nothing special."

- **Should or Must Statements.** Applying rigid rules of behavior to self or others, frequently resulting in anger, guilt, or disappointment.
  Example: "I should always be there for my friends, otherwise I am a lousy friend" (setting an unrealistic standard and not leaving room for extenuating circumstances).

- **Labeling.** Putting a label on self or others based on a single situation.
  Example: "I am so stupid; I couldn't even clear a simple test."

- **Personalization.** Blaming yourself or taking responsibility for external events.
  Example: "I should have seen this coming."

I mentioned early on that it is hard to identify these errors in your thinking but while reading some of these, were you able to relate to any? Can you recognize some of the errors you make in your daily life? Let us look at our example from the previous day. This was the thoughts section: "My son would be so upset. His teachers would think less of me. I am such an incompetent father."

Do any cognitive distortions apply to these thoughts? His teachers would think less of me: Jumping to conclusions. I am such an incompetent father: Overgeneralization, Labeling. As evident, cognitive distortions hide in seemingly innocuous thoughts. This is why it is important to be aware of and recognize these errors in your own thinking.

ACTIVITY:
Recognize Cognitive Distortions

Write down the errors you feel you end up making in your daily life. Look back at your journal from yesterday. In your thoughts section, do you identify any cognitive distortions? Continue doing the Activity from Day 1 with this addition.

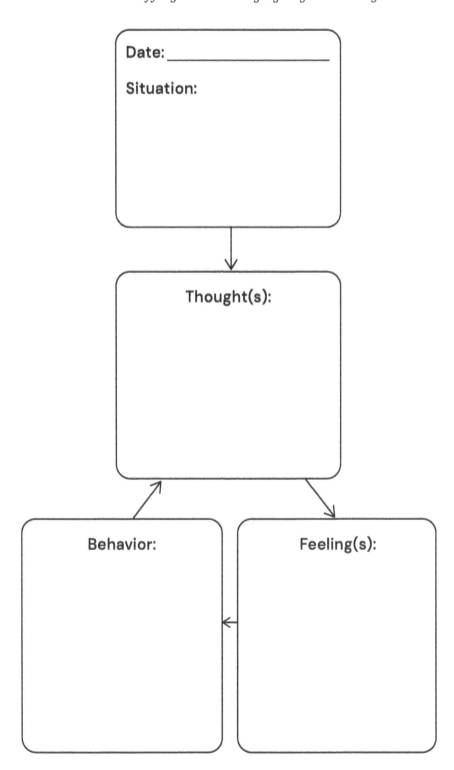

Identify the cognitive distortion if any:

_____

_____

If you'd like to reuse this template to recognize other distortions in the future, you can do so by accessing the pdf available via the QR code, or by using this link: *https://bit.ly/28-cbt*

Analyzing Your Cognitive Distortions

Were you able to identify some of your cognitive distortions?

ACTIVITY:
Identify Cognitive Distortions

Cognitive Distortions
1.
2.
3.
4.
5.

Let's analyze them. For each cognitive distortion, are you able to identify a pattern? Ask yourself these questions.

- Does this distortion show up in particular areas of my life?
- Does it come up with certain people or situations?
- Which kinds of situations trigger it?
- How does this distortion affect my feelings and behaviors?
- Is there a long-term impact of this cognitive distortion?

Let me give you an example.
Distortion: Discounting the positive

Does this distortion show up in particular areas of my life? I often discount my professional achievements.

Does it come up with certain people or situations? I find myself doing it more with my manager.

Which kinds of situations trigger it? Whenever my boss appreciates something I have achieved, my instant reaction is to discount or undermine it by saying it wasn't a big deal.

How does this distortion affect my feelings and behaviors? When I think in this manner, it is hard for me to take the credit I deserve for it. It seems like I am always working towards endless goals, but I never feel satisfied or fulfilled because I don't acknowledge either my efforts or my achievements. As a result, I don't feel I have done anything to be proud of.

Is there a long-term impact of this cognitive distortion? This sets me on a constant hamster-wheel, trying to get somewhere but never actually acknowledging having reached there. It affects my self-esteem; my manager might stop praising me as I never seem to be able to take it well. I would continue to feel dissatisfied at work which may eventually affect my workplace motivation.

ACTIVITY:
Analyze Cognitive Distortions

Go ahead and do this exercise for one of the cognitive distortions you have identified so far in your thinking.

Distortion 1:

Does this distortion show up in particular areas of my life?

_____

_____

Does it come up with certain people or situations?

_____

_____

Which kinds of situations trigger it?

_____

_____

How does this distortion affect my feelings and behaviors?

_____

_____

Is there a long-term impact of this cognitive distortion?

_____

_____

Also, make sure to continue logging down daily instances, you can use the following graphic to do so.

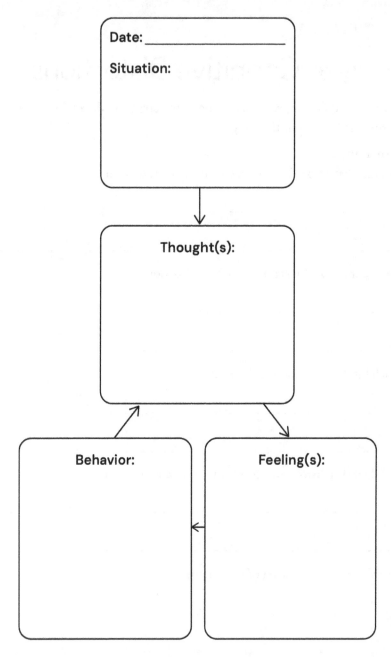

Date: _____

Situation:

Thought(s):

Behavior:

Feeling(s):

Identify the cognitive distortion if any:

_____

_____

DAY 8:

Challenging Your Cognitive Distortions

Now that you have an idea of the most common cognitive distortions you engage in and the pattern they appear in, we need to challenge them in order to reduce their impact on your daily life. Let's see how we can do that. Pick a thought that you have identified where you noticed a cognitive distortion. Now ask yourself some questions to challenge the validity of these thoughts. You can easily remember these questions using the acronym, CRAFTED to remind yourself our thoughts aren't always the true representation of reality, sometimes they are 'crafted' by us.

C: Challenge the thought. Do I have any evidence that my thought is true?

R: Is it Realistic? Will this likely happen?

A: Assumptions I'm making, or alternate explanations that might apply to this situation.

F: Friendly advice I'd give to someone dealing with this.

T: Time in 6 months to a year, how will I feel about this situation?

E: Do I have any evidence that is contrary to my thought?

D: Different perspectives to see this situation.

Using the example from previous days, let's try to ask the above questions.

Thought: My son would be so upset. His teachers would think less of me. I am such an incompetent father.

C: Challenge the thought: I am never late for the pickup, so my son is bound to be upset as he is unfamiliar with this situation.

R: Is it realistic? The realistic worst possible outcome of this situation: my wife being mad at me for picking up our son late. The probability of that happening is around 40%.

A: Assumptions I'm making: In thinking these thoughts, I was making the assumption that my son would be all alone at the school, his teachers would have to stay 10 minutes extra, waiting for me, and that this is an unpardonable mistake, even when it is maybe the second time in 2 years that I have been delayed.

F: If a friend of mine was thinking this thought, I would tell him to go easy on himself. He was doing the best he can, and it is all right if he got delayed one time. It was not in his control. It is a rare occurrence, and I am sure both his son and his teachers would be understanding and considerate. I would remind him what a wonderful Dad he is.

T: Time: I would not even remember this situation in 6 months or a year. I don't think it is significant in the longer term.

E: Evidence against thought: I mostly pick my son right on time and I spend good quality time with him every day. His teachers are always polite, friendly, and courteous towards me. When I apologized for the delay, they took it well and didn't show any signs of being irritated with me. My son was playing with one of his friends whose mother was delayed in the pick-up and he didn't even notice I was late. He was enthusiastic while telling me about the game he and his friend were playing when I arrived.

The teachers were inconvenienced, but they would probably not hold it against me as I always pick up my son on time. My son might be upset but he would forget about it in some time. I can also let him know that the reason I got delayed was that my presentation ran over and despite my best attempts, it took those extra 10 minutes to wrap it up. I had immediately informed the teachers about the delay over the phone, even before the school let out.

D: Different Perspectives: To look at this situation differently, I acknowledge my mistake while also considering that there were factors beyond my control. I did my best, considering the circumstances. As it is a one-off thing, I will not continue to hold myself accountable or berate myself over it.

This last question leads to a reframing of the situation and working on tweaking your thinking accordingly while keeping all relevant facts in mind. Let us look at another example to understand this process better. In this example let's say a girl named Linda has a friend who set up a date for her. On the evening of the date, Linda finds herself feeling nervous and thinking anxiously.

Thought: My date will find me boring or awkward. It will be just like the last date where I fumbled to find the right words. I will make a spectacle of myself. What's the point of even going?'

C Challenge The Thought: This happened on my last date. I didn't even know what to say. It was terrible.

R Is it Realistic: There's a 50/50 chance of my date finding me odd if I'm awkward and fumble my words.

A Assumptions & Alternative Explanations: I am assuming that a repeat of last time would happen.

F Friendly Advice: I'd tell them, 'Just go. If things don't go well, cite a reason and leave. You'll likely never see this person again."

T How Will This Feel Over Time: I may feel bad about it for a few weeks but in 6 months or a year, I think it may not matter much.

E Evidence Against Thought: Apart from the last date, it's not common for me. I'm fine with my friends, and when I feel comfortable.

D Different Perspectives: There might be a chance that this wouldn't be a repeat of my last date. Things might actually go well.

ACTIVITY:
Challenging Cognitive Distortions

Now try challenging your own distortions using the prompts below.

Thought:_____

_____

C Challenge The Thought:_____

_____

R Is it Realistic:_____

_____

A Assumptions & Alternative Explanations:_____

_____

F Friendly Advice:_____

_____

T How Will This Feel Over Time:_____

_____

E Evidence Against Thought:_____

_____

D Different Perspectives:_____

_____

After you have completed this exercise with a few of these thoughts, now add some more columns to your daily journaling.

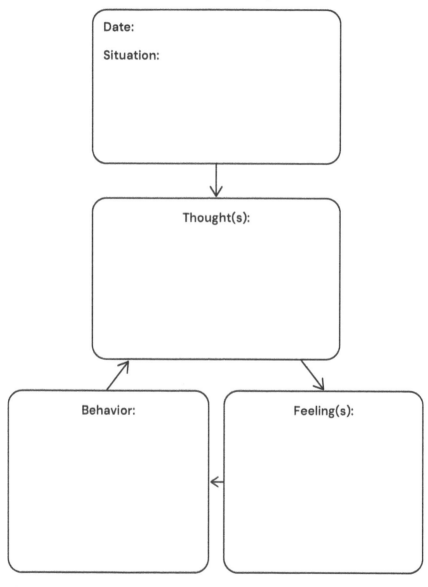

Identify the cognitive distortion if any:

_____

_____

Evidence For:

_____

_____

Evidence Against:

_____

_____

Alternative Thought:

_____

_____

If you'd like to reuse this template for journaling in the future, you can do so by accessing the pdf available via the QR code, or by using this link: *https://bit.ly/28-cbt*

Today we have started to target your cognitive distortions. Remember, these thoughts come automatically to you and are resistant to change. It is not possible to change them overnight. What we are trying here is to help you learn to challenge these thoughts, to test their validity, to be your own advocate, to find evidence and rationality in your thoughts. However, this activity needs to be repeated over and over again with every thought in different scenarios before they start to crumble. The key is to be kind and compassionate with yourself and not be frustrated every time a thought comes back with a, 'Oh no, not again!' exclamation.

By using the above techniques, we are not ignoring these thoughts (distraction only works in the short-term) but eradicating them from their roots. The repetition of the above process would help you notice a gradual shift in how you observe situations and how you react to them based on your thoughts about the situation. Tomorrow, we will focus on how to reframe these thoughts in a positive manner.

PART 3

Reframing and Taking Action

In the last four days, you have understood the principles of CBT and identified and challenged your cognitive distortions. For the next 4 days, you will be testing the accuracy of your thoughts and learning to positively reframe your thoughts. You will also be reducing avoidant behaviors and engaging in enjoyable activities.

Positive reframing would allow you to look at your thoughts from a balanced perspective. By being able to challenge and test your thoughts, you will arrive at a healthier and realistic outlook. In order to test out your thoughts in real life situations, you will be carrying out behavioral experiments. Further, employing the behavioral component of CBT, you will be working on reducing avoidance behaviors. Anxiety can often result in avoiding certain situations or behaviors which helps in the short-term to curb anxiety but does not reduce anxiety in the longer-term. By engaging in enjoyable activities like reading a book, going for a picnic, or walking your dog, you will be able to assert a sense of self-control and pave your way to a purposeful life.

On day 13, you will be taking a closer look at your lifestyle habits and checking what needs to change for you to feel healthy, both physically and mentally. Establishing healthy lifestyle habits would positively impact your emotional well-being. With the help of small improvements, like having a fixed sleep-wake up routine or eating healthy, you will be able to build a plan for long-term change.

Day 14 will introduce techniques for time management. If you struggle with anxiety or low self-esteem, you might be spending a lot of time overthinking and it might take you longer to get started on goals. This section will help you prioritize, avoid distractions, and schedule goals in a realistic manner, promoting self-care and productivity.

We will be doing a mid-program check-in, reflection, and review on Day 15 to ensure you are on the right path. This day would involve you acknowledging your progress so far, checking if your goals are still relevant, recognizing the obstacles you have encountered, and what would help you with them moving forward. This would be a time to reassess goals, tweak any if needed, and identify areas you need more or less support with. This mid-program check-in is important to help you understand how your goals may change with time and it's important to remain flexible and open-minded to make modifications, to ensure you make the most of this workbook.

Learning Positive Reframing

You have been identifying your thoughts in intense situations for a few days now. This should have given you some idea of your thought patterns. However, considering it is a short time to unravel all maladaptive thought patterns, here's a checklist to identify any negative automatic thoughts that didn't come up yet.

- No one likes me.
- I am not lovable.
- I am not good enough.
- I am a failure.
- I always make a mess of things.
- I am not a good mother/ father/ sister/ brother/ husband/ wife/ friend.
- I cannot deal with this.

Can you relate to any of these? For Laura, every time someone said 'no' to her, it felt like a rejection. When a friend couldn't meet her because her work commitments came up, Laura felt ignored. She thought 'no one loves me, even my friend didn't make time for me.'

ACTIVITY:
Negative Automatic Thoughts

Negative Automatic Thoughts
1.
2.
3.
4.
5.
6.
7.
8.
9.
10.

Being aware of these commonly occurring negative automatic thoughts would help you dispute them better. Use techniques from the previous days to challenge them. You can see an example of this process, and then try it for yourself in the following activity.

Negative Automatic Thought: No one likes me

_____

_____

Evidence For Thought:	**Evidence Against Thought:**
My friend didn't meet me.	My friend has, in the past,
	always made time for me. She
	has been there when I have
	needed her. I also have other
	friends who care for me and
	love me.

Alternative Thought: My friends like me even though sometimes life situations may make it feel like they are not there for me.

_____

ACTIVITY:
Thought Journal

Negative Automatic Thought: _____

_____

_____

Evidence For Thought:	**Evidence Against Thought:**
_____	_____
_____	_____
_____	_____
_____	_____
_____	_____
_____	_____

Alternative Thought: _____

_____

_____

Continue practicing these exercises over the next few days until you become so good at it that you are able to do these steps in your mind without having to put them to paper. We did some positive reframing yesterday. Let's try that again today. Think of or look back at your worksheets from Day 5, 6, or 7 to identify a challenging situation that has come up recently. Identify the negative automatic thought. Now try to reframe the situation using the following questions:

- Did I learn something from this situation?

- How can I utilize this learning in the future?

- Was there anything positive about the situation?

Spend some time reflecting on this positive reframing of the situation.

- Does it make you look at the situation differently?

- How does it affect your feelings?

Once again taking the example we have been working with, let's do this exercise.

Positive Reframing: I learnt from this situation that a lot of my worries about the situation did not actually occur in reality. I spent a lot of time putting myself down even though it was a one-off situation and everyone including my son, his teachers, and my wife did not make a big deal of it.

In the future, I can try to look at a larger perspective and be kind to myself in difficult situations. I can try not to keep my presentations closer to my son's pick-up time or inform my colleagues in advance of the time I would have to leave by. I can also try to seek my wife's help in these circumstances. The situation made me realize how critical I am of myself and that I need to cut myself some slack. It also reminded me that I can always ask for help, which is something I hesitate to do. I am able to look at the situation differently now. It makes me feel better about myself. I do not hold onto the guilt I was experiencing earlier.

ACTIVITY:
Positive Reframing

Now do this by yourself for a challenging situation you've encountered in the past.

Challenging situation:

_____

_____

Negative automatic thought:

_____

_____

Did I learn something from this situation?

_____

_____

How can I utilize this learning in the future?

_____

_____

Was there anything positive about the situation?

_____

_____

Does it make me look at the situation differently?

_____

_____

How does it affect my feelings?

_____

_____

Today, you focused on picking apart your unhelpful thoughts and looking at them from a balanced, rational perspective. By practicing this, you are making the shift from being stuck in a loop of cognitive errors to a mindset that helps you grow and move forward. Remember like other skills you are learning through this 28-day workbook, this skill also takes time to master. Be kind and compassionate with your pace. Instead of being frustrated, gently remind yourself every time you catch a cognitive distortion and lead it to the place of positive reframing.

DAY 10:

Testing the Accuracy of Your Thoughts

Now that you have had time to work on your thoughts, let us put them into practice. These practical scenarios are called Behavioral Experiments. In order to further reduce cognitive distortions and strengthen our alternative adaptive ways of thinking, it is important to test them out in real life.

The first step is to identify a negative automatic thought that can be tested behaviorally. For someone grappling with anxiety, this could be a thought like, "If I ask a stranger for help with directions, they will think I am wasting their time, and they will be annoyed with me." Let's design an experiment to test out this thought. This would entail going out and asking a stranger for help with directions. But before you do that, write down in as much detail as possible what you think would ensue and how others will react. Then carry out the experiment as planned and make notes of your observations. Be in touch with your feelings during and after carrying out the experiment. Once the experiment is over, compare your predictions with the actual outcome. Were your predictions accurate? Did others react as per your predictions? Reframe your thoughts based on the outcome.

In this example, Leah asked a stranger for help with directions. She was very anxious, and it took her a few tries before she could muster up the courage. She asked one of the ladies who was waiting for her bus at the stop. The lady appeared kind and she calmly and helpfully told Leah how to get to her destination. She was pleasant and she smiled when Leah thanked her. Leah felt a sense of relief wash all over her once the experiment was complete. It was difficult for her to put herself out there, struggling with a fear of being rejected. But when she compared the outcome with her predictions, she was able to see how she had magnified the situation in her mind and attached negative connotations to it while in reality, it turned out to be a pleasant experience. The lady did not appear agitated, instead she seemed almost eager to help Leah out. Leah reframed her thought, "Most people are nice and willing to help another person out. My asking for directions is not troublesome for most people."

ACTIVITY:
Try a Behavioral Experiment

Now go ahead and try out a behavioral experiment with one of your thoughts.

Identify a negative automatic thought that can be tested behaviorally:

_____

_____

Design the experiment:

_____

_____

Write down in as much detail as possible what you think would ensue and how others will react:

_____

_____

Carry out the experiment as planned and make notes of your observations:

_____

_____

Were your predictions accurate? Did others react as per your predictions?:

_____

_____

Reframe your thought based on the outcome:

_____

_____

In this manner, you can plan out other behavioral experiments to aid with reframing your thoughts. Today, you have worked on moving beyond the face value of accepting your thoughts and tested them out through behavioral experiments. When you actively test out your thoughts, it makes it easier to see the faults in them which enables you to let go of cognitive distortions and reframe your thoughts in an adaptive manner.

DAY 11:

Overcoming Avoidance

There is a tendency to avoid certain behaviors even though they may be beneficial currently or in the longer term. This avoidance may turn to procrastination and with it, comes guilt, frustration, and disappointment. Rita was feeling overwhelmed with the deadlines at work. In order to find more time to work, she decided to skip her daily practice of yoga. She used that hour to work. The realization that she now had an extra hour to devote to work felt like a relief. She continued this for 3 more days before she felt resentful towards her work. She was irritable, tired, and stayed in bed longer than usual, which delayed her at work.

If you notice in your daily life, there is a trigger (work demands) which leads you to engage in avoidance (stop practicing yoga) that provides short-term relief (more time to work) but is followed by an adverse impact in the long term (resentment, irritability).

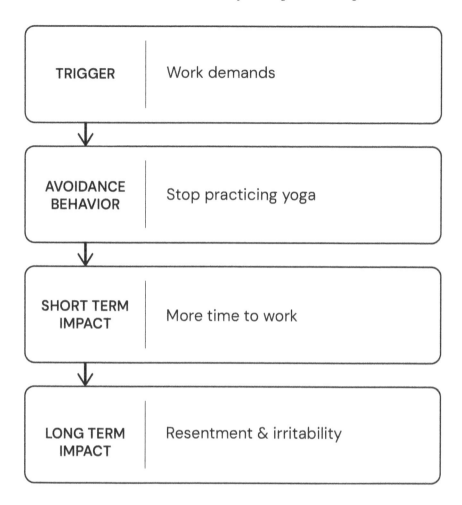

TRIGGER	Work demands
AVOIDANCE BEHAVIOR	Stop practicing yoga
SHORT TERM IMPACT	More time to work
LONG TERM IMPACT	Resentment & irritability

Avoidance may seem to be working but it has an adverse impact over time.

Activity:
Identify Avoidance Behaviors

During a stressful or demanding situation, which behaviors do you end up avoiding?

Example:

- Ordering in instead of cooking at home
- Delaying doing laundry
- Canceling socialization plans
- Procrastinating work

Make your list of Avoidance Behaviors:

1.	
2.	
3.	
4.	
5.	
6.	
7.	
8.	

Activity:
Avoidance Behavior Process

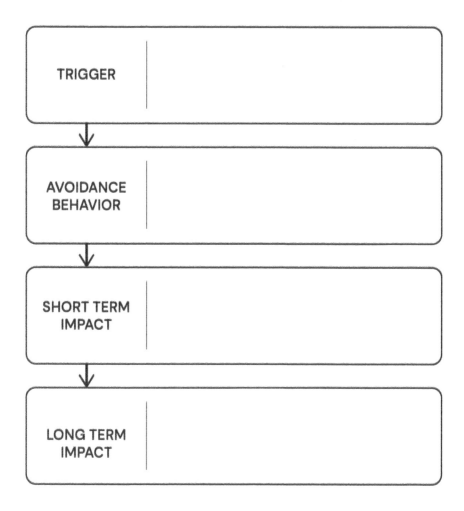

TRIGGER

AVOIDANCE BEHAVIOR

SHORT TERM IMPACT

LONG TERM IMPACT

Think back to the times you avoided these behaviors. How did it affect your mood and behavior over time?

Example: Not having to worry about doing laundry was great but eventually I had to stress about what to wear to work the next day. Then I was worried if it would dry in time for my work by morning. It was an unnecessary stress that I felt could have been avoided.

Activity:
Identify Your Feelings Post Avoidance Behaviors

Avoiding doing

_____

made me feel

_____

_____

_____

_____

Avoiding doing

_____

made me feel

_____

_____

_____

Once you are able to reflect on how avoidance only works in the short-term while being harmful in the long-term, what can you tell yourself to make sure you don't avoid the behavior?

Example: 'I know not doing yoga would give me another hour to work on this, but it would also make me miserable in the long-term. Yoga is my way of destressing and caring for my body and mind. It helps me focus more and function better during my work hours.'

ACTIVITY:
Write a Motivating Statement

Try writing down a statement that would help you remember why you don't want to avoid doing a certain Activity.

"I realize

_____

                                                    "

_____

The next step for reducing avoidance is to take small, achievable steps towards the avoided activity with the longer-term goal of achieving it.

Example: **Avoided activity – Cooking**
Steps to Take:

1. Make grocery list

2. Buy groceries

3. Decide what to cook

4. Cook

Take it slow, step by step. Schedule one step at a time. Find a rewarding activity to follow up the step with. The idea is to only focus on the next step and not be overwhelmed by the larger goal.

ACTIVITY:
Reducing Avoidance

Avoided Activity:

_____

_____

_____

_____

Steps To Take:

Step 1) _____

Step 2) _____

Step 3) _____

Step 4) _____

Engaging in Enjoyable Activities

While it is important to work on goals every day, it is equally important to find time in your day for activities you enjoy doing. Jot down 5 activities that bring you joy or used to make you happy. Think of something that makes you feel a sense of accomplishment.

Example:

1. Reading a book
2. Going for a walk in the park.
3. Playing with my dog.
4. Decluttering my table.
5. Listening to music.

ACTIVITY:

Write Your Joyful List

1.	
2.	
3.	
4.	
5.	

If you are already finding time for all these in your daily life, that's amazing! If not, pick one activity from the above list that you can do today or tomorrow. Yet again, make it a SMART goal.

Example: I will read 3 pages of this book today at 9pm before bed.
Notice it is a SMART goal. It is specific, measurable, achievable, realistic, and time-bound.

ACTIVITY:

Make Goals for Upcoming Days

Over the next few days, see if you can do more activities from your top 5 list. You don't need to do them all in one day, every day. Depending on your mood and availability of time, you can alternate between them or do what seems best when. Remember these activities make you happy, they should not feel burdensome.

Which joyful activity will you engage in tomorrow?

I will

_____

Which joyful activity will you engage in the day after?

I will

_____

Like the activities we avoid, we even face obstacles to engaging in joyful activities. Identify the challenges you face. What stops you from spending time doing your joyful activity? Della loved reading. She had a huge bookshelf in her room that she often found herself staring at. At one point in time, she used to read 5 books a month. But for the last 6 months, she had not even picked up a book. When asked why she hadn't read during the last few months, she cited a lack of time and motivation. "It is easier to just watch TV or scroll through my phone instead of reading and then it's time for bed," she said. "I do miss my reading time though."

Sounds familiar? It is very easy to get sucked into scrolling mindlessly on your phone or passively watching Netflix. These activities supply us with a neurotransmitter called dopamine which makes us feel good, thus, making it hard to do activities that we actually enjoy. Let's identify what are the obstacles you face in doing something enjoyable.

Activity:
Identify Obstacles

Obstacles:

_____

_____

_____

_____

Proposed Solutions:

1) _____

2) _____

3) _____

Now, propose solutions on how to overcome them. For Della, in order to overcome her obstacles of time and motivation. She decided to schedule 30 minutes of reading time in the calendar before bed. She said she would put away her phone and switch off the TV half an hour before bed. She also planned her next read and kept it by her bedside for easy access. She ensured she had a reading light by her bed to engage in this activity.

ACTIVITY:
Steps to Overcoming Obstacles

Fill your proposed solutions in the diagram under the label "proposed solutions" after the obstacles you wrote. Make sure to schedule these activities in your calendar to remind you, the first few days.

Building Lasting, Healthy Habits

Having healthy lifestyle habits are a must for maintaining physical and psychological health. These habits include eating, sleeping, and exercising. When incorporated with a balance into your daily routine, they have a good impact on your mood, energy levels, and overall health. All of us eat healthy at times or have a good night's sleep once in a while. But it is the consistency that makes the difference. Having a daily routine that balances it all would add to your quality of life.

Sleep Hygiene

Having a restful sleep is not only good for your body but also for your mind. It helps you process memories better, regulates your emotions, and ensures more focus.

Here are some of the basics of sleep hygiene.

- **Have a consistent sleep schedule.** Sleep and wake up at the same time to regulate your internal body clock. Even on weekends, try not to go too astray from your sleep-wake timings.

- **Slow down before bedtime.** Try to put devices (phone, laptop, TV) away at least half an hour before bed. Have a bedtime routine. It could be listening to music, reading a book, doing slow stretches, meditation, or even your skincare routine.

- **Find a comfortable sleeping environment.** Ensure the room is dark, the temperature is moderate (not too cold or warm), and it is quiet and calm.

- **Track your sleep pattern.** There are countless apps out there to jot down your sleep-wake timings, and quality of sleep. You can also use a sleep journal. This record would help you understand what affects your sleep and thereby take steps to ensure better sleep quality.

- **Ensure a comfortable sleeping surface.** Unless you travel often for work or otherwise, you would likely be sleeping in the same bed each night. It is important to ensure the mattress and pillows are as per your comfort. If you feel like your back or neck aches on waking up, you might need to change the mattress or pillow or check your sleeping posture. Use soft, comfortable bed sheets.

- **Bed is for sleeping.** Try not to be on your bed unless planning to sleep. Sit on a chair or sofa until it's bedtime. This helps your body and mind understand the connection and makes it easier and quicker for you to fall asleep.

- **Dietary considerations.** The last meal before bed should be a light one. If your stomach feels too heavy, it will be difficult to have a restful sleep. A cup of warm milk or green tea before bed might help lull you to sleep. Be mindful of not drinking a lot of water a few hours before bedtime because this will lead to multiple bathroom breaks at night disrupting your sleep.

Sleep Journal

Example:
Time I went to bed: 10pm
Time I woke up: 6am
Quality of sleep (score from 1=very poor to 10=very restful): 5

Possible reasons for sleep quality:

- I had a stressful meeting coming up today, couldn't sleep for the longest time.

- Cramps during my menstrual cycle woke me up in the middle of the night.

- Loud sounds from my neighbor woke me up earlier than expected.

- I ate a heavy meal the night before and couldn't sleep because of the stomachache.

ACTIVITY:
Now Fill This Tomorrow Morning

Time I went to bed:	
Time I woke up:	
Quality of sleep (score from 1=very poor to 10=very restful):	
Possible reasons for sleep quality:	

Physical Fitness

Regular physical exercise improves your stamina, mood, and overall health. Instead of thinking of having to take out several hours of your time each week, focus on consistency and habit. You don't have to exercise 2 hours a day. 30 minutes of exercise 5 days a week on a consistent, regular basis is great!

Establishing an Exercise Routine

- **Find something that is enjoyable.** Do you like going for walks? Playing tennis with a friend? Swimming? Learning a new sport? Dancing? If it is something you enjoy doing, you are more likely to carve out time and be consistent with it. If you join a gym but do not enjoy the gym environment, you will find yourself missing several days eventually.

- **Make SMART goals.** Once again, if you dive headlong into something, it will work well for a few initial days and then you will tire yourself out and completely stop. The key is to start small and find consistency. If you don't exercise at all, start with 20 minutes of exercise 3 days a week. Do it for 2 weeks before you increase either the time or the frequency.

- **Ask yourself important questions before you begin?** Why do I want to do this? What is my motivation? Is this important to me, why? Am I looking to achieve something, what is it? Example- I want to do yoga thrice a week because I want to work on my flexibility; I want to do more cardio exercises to improve my stamina; I want to move my body daily (by walking, running, cardio etc.) with a focus on losing weight and having more energy and feeling fit.

- **Find innovative solutions.** If you are strapped for time and cannot carve out an exercise schedule, think small. Can you take stairs instead of the elevator? Can you get off a stop earlier from the bus and walk the rest of the way home? Can you walk to the grocery store instead of taking your car? Can you stretch 10mins, first thing in the morning? Can you exercise on the weekend if that's the only time you have? Can you go for a 15 min walk post your lunch at the office?

- **Seek accountability.** Sometimes it's hard to get started. Try to find a partner, a friend, a neighbor, a colleague. If someone already has a schedule, it's easier for you to join in. If your neighbor takes her dog for a walk every evening, ask if she will be okay with you joining in. Ask your friend if you can join him at the gym. And if nothing works out, ask a friend to check-in with your new exercise schedule to keep you accountable.

- **Track Progress.** Tracking progress can be motivating but make sure it doesn't become too rigid. You do not need to check your weight each day. Schedule measurements at no less than 10 days apart. You can measure your weight, body fat percentage, body measurements, etc. Another reliable measure is what you observe each day. When you are able to do 10 pushups instead of 7 the week before; or when you are able to hold your toe during a yoga posture when you could only grab the ankle

5 days back. These are all signs of progress. Make sure to acknowledge and appreciate them before moving onto the next goal.

Getting started with exercise

Example:

Chosen Exercise: Running

Frequency and Intensity: Start with 15 minutes, 3 days a week

Why do I want to do this? I want to run a 10k in 3 months

How will I ensure consistency? Set a reminder, carve out time, prepare my running clothes and shoes the night before, prepare my running playlist, tell a friend about my intention, sign up for the marathon.

How will I track my progress? Journal about how my body feels after the run, ability to cover longer distances in shorter time comparatively.

Schedule for next 3 months: Increase duration by 15 minutes each week until I reach the 10k point; increase number of days to 4 and then 5 with 2 weeks gap between each increase.

Activity:
Write Down Your Intentions

Chosen Exercise:

_____

Frequency and Intensity:

_____

_____

Why do I want to do this?:

_____

_____

How will I ensure consistency?:

_____

_____

How will I track my progress?:

_____

_____

Schedule for next 3 months:

_____

_____

Healthy Diet

Eating a balanced diet is good for your gut, body, and overall health. The focus is on balance and moderation. Keeping a strict diet is not sustainable in the long-term while eating out every day is not going to aid your physical health. It's important to find what is the right balance for you.

- **Incorporate balanced meals in your diet.** Focusing on one food type is not beneficial. You need to eat vegetables, fruits, grains, proteins, and healthy fats for a balanced diet.

- **Avoid undereating or overeating.** When we are eating while watching TV or reading a book, it is hard to keep track of the quantity. Also, if you are distracted, your mind and body doesn't register the fact of eating. Being mindfully present while eating helps you understand when you are full and prevents you from overeating. The key is to eat slowly, focus on your food (its color, taste, smell, texture) and pay attention to the body signals of hunger or feeling satiated.

- **Drink enough water.** Sometimes thirst signals make you feel like you're hungry. It is thus important to ensure you are well hydrated. Aim at drinking 8-12 glasses of water depending on the weather and your activity levels. If required, put 'drink water' reminders at regular intervals on your phone or grab a big bottle of water to take to work with the intention that you should finish all the water in it before heading home.

- **Limit foods that are not good for you.** Avoid processed, sugary, fried foods as much as possible. Occasional intake of these foods is fine but don't make it a habit. Make it a habit to check ingredients at the grocery store. If it has sugar or an unknown substance, check if there is an alternative to that food item. As a rule, the longer a product remains fresh (farther 'use before' date), the chances are the more processed it is, except food items that are pickled, fermented, or sun dried etc.

- **Reduce eating out.** It might be hard to find time to plan or cook every day. Take out time on the weekend to plan and meal prep for the week. Think of quick healthy recipes that can be rustled up in no time. Roasted veggies or air-fried tofu might be some good options to pair with a side of rice, bread, or meat.

Diet Journal

Example:
I want to eat more of: vegetables, fruits, fibrous food.
I want to eat less of: processed foods, fried food items, sugary items/ desserts.
Glasses of water: 8
Meal prep ideas: Zucchini pasta; Braised Tofu; Green papaya salad; Quinoa with roasted veggies.

ACTIVITY:
Your Diet Goals

I want to eat more of:

_____

_____

I want to eat less of:

_____

_____

Glasses of water:

_____

Meal prep ideas:

_____

_____

Now that you have plans to work on establishing these healthy routine habits, let's bring it all together for you to have it all in one place.

Sleeping time:
Wake-up time:
Exercise of Choice:
Frequency and intensity:
Daily intake of water:
Eat more of:
Eat less of:

Once you begin to follow the above plan, keep a note of how it feels for you and adjust till it feels just right. If it feels too much to exercise 3 days a week, switch to 2 days a week instead. If drinking 8 glasses of water per day feels unachievable, stick to 6 to begin with. If cooking 3 meals a day is not possible, start with 2 meals and try to find a healthy alternative to eat outside or order in, for the third meal. Remember we want to develop a habit that is consistent over the long-term. If it feels too restrictive, you will not be able to stick to it.

DAY 14:

Learning Time Management

As you are establishing all these healthy habits from the last few days, one of the biggest obstacles you will encounter is to find time to schedule everything in your busy life. Poor time management often leads to feeling overwhelmed, anxious, or irritated, which, in turn, exacerbates the cognitive distortions. By learning to manage time well, CBT helps you to create realistic and achievable schedules, thereby reducing unnecessary stress. This would ensure you have the bandwidth to challenge negative thinking and continue to work towards your goals.

Sheena, a former client of mine, was an aspirational marketing profession-al. Her day was spent catching up on endless meetings and work. But she also wanted to have time to exercise, meet friends, learn to dance salsa, and get into bed at a decent hour. Now, at a first glance, all these seem like reasonable and logical expectations to have of one's schedule. But if you have ever tried to fit a zillion things in your day and failed, you will know that logic doesn't always translate well to practice.

Time management, thus, is an extremely important skill to learn to:

- Make the most of your day.

- Avoid distractions.

- Work towards your goals.

- Prevent burnout.

- Stop procrastination.

- Achieve your goals.

- Reduce stress.

The first week of her new schedule, Sheena spent 9am to 7pm at her work, then she went to her salsa class, met friends at 9, gym at 10:30, and finally crashed at midnight. She did it for 4 consecutive days before giving it all up because she was tired and frustrated. She wanted to do it all but realized it was too much to ask of herself. How could Sheena have managed her time better? Were her goals realistic? Let's focus on you for a bit before I go back to my sessions with Sheena and what we figured out together. Before we get to learning techniques of time management, it would be helpful to assess and recognize how you spend time currently. Think back to a typical weekday for you.

ACTIVITY:
Assess Your Daily Activities

Jot down activities in your typical day that you spend time on-

Example of activities in a typical day may look like-

- Brush, freshen up

- Bathing

- Ironing work clothes

- Getting Ready

- Preparing and eating meals

- Commute to and from work

- Work meetings

- Work

- Gym

- Shower

- TV

- Spending time on phone

- Calling friends/ meeting friends

Activities in a typical day
1.
2.
3.
4.
5.
6.
7.
8.
9.
10.
11.
12.

Now if you were to divide the above list into tasks that you find productive which help you meet your goals, and those that consume your time but don't add any value, what would that look like?

Example:

Productive	Not adding Value
Brush, freshen up	TV (Binge watching)
Bathing	Using phone before bed
Ironing work clothes	
Getting Ready	
Preparing and eating meals	
Commute to and from work	
Work meetings	
Working	
Gym	
Shower	
Calling friends	

Now, this is a quite subjective activity based on your definition of productivity. For example, for some of you, commuting to and from work might seem unproductive but there might be no way to avoid or change that. To others, maybe meeting friends isn't the best use of time. Go with what seems to be right by your definition of productivity or addition of value.

ACTIVITY:
Value of Daily Activities

Productive	Not adding Value

Based on the above activity, you might be able to have a better idea of what can be improved in your day to find time for other activities that might be more valuable to you. Keep in mind, the idea is not to cut off activities that are unproductive. Watching TV and spending time on your phone is not the problem. But you might want to take a closer look at what you are watching/ doing on your phone and for how long, and if the frequency, duration, or quality of it needs to change. Maybe watching TV is your idea of relaxing after a long day and if you are watching for half an hour or an hour on a weekday, that's not a problem. But if you are binge watching until 1am in the morning, maybe that needs to change because then you don't wake up in time to go to the gym which is an important goal for you. It's all about finding the right balance for yourself.

Now let's learn some techniques to better manage your time. It is a well-known fact that with the usage of phones, our attention span has gone for a toss[5]. The Pomodoro technique works with your limited attention span while discouraging procrastination by getting you going with the task[6]. This is how it works.

Pomodoro Technique

Break your tasks in 25-minute intervals which are followed by a 5-minute break.

- Pick a task.
- Set your timer for 25 minutes.
- Focus and work.
- Take a 5-minute break.
- Back to task.
- Repeat these 3 more times before taking a longer break of 20-30 minutes.
- Repeat the entire process, based on time and energy.

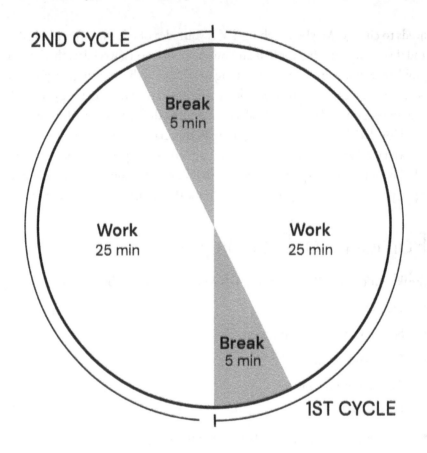

Now, remember the mistake most people make is pick up their phones in the 5-minute break. Believe me, if you do that, the break will get much longer. Decide your break activity in advance. Am I going to drink a glass or water, or make a coffee, or do 10 sit ups, or make that dinner reservation, or just close my eyes, or meditate? The idea is to choose to do nothing or a small activity that will not last for more than 5 minutes. If you end up choosing a stimulating activity like watching a YouTube short, a reel on Instagram, or calling a friend, you will miss that 5-minute window, and it will get difficult to return to the task.

ACTIVITY:
Applying Pomodoro Technique

Can you think of a task you can attempt your first pomodoro with? Write it here.

_____

_____

If you are someone who makes daily to-do lists, think back to your last one. Those 5 or 10 things on your list. How do you tackle them, in which order? What most people end up doing is checking off the easy, quick ones off the list first. It is so gratifying to see 3 things checked off before it's 11am, right? But does it mean you put off doing that one difficult thing day after day on your daily to-do until you either give up on it or the deadline comes to push you through? Yeah, we have all been there. How to get out of this rut? Here's how. Use the Eisenhower Matrix which has been proven to help individuals reduce distractions and be more productive[7]. This matrix helps you prioritize your tasks based on how important and urgent they are instead of how quickly they can get done.

Eisenhower Matrix

	Urgent	**Not Urgent**
Important	Do these first (Example – task with an immediate work deadline)	Schedule these to work on later (Example- buy a new shirt)
Not Important	Try to delegate these (Example- reply to an email)	Eliminate or postpone (Example – pick up a new set of curtains)

ACTIVITY:
Use the Eisenhower Matrix

To make the best use of this matrix, right after you make your daily to-do list, divide those tasks in this matrix and then work on them in the order of priority. You can also assign the urgent, important tasks during the most focused time of your day (for most people, this is in the morning), and assign the urgent, not important, or low-attention-needing tasks post-lunch (which is the time when most people have lower attention span and energy).

	Urgent	Not Urgent
Important		
Not Important		

   The last time management technique that I want to introduce to you is the Two Minute Rule. Think of all the emails you open up, read, and mark as unread or put it on your task list to do later. The Two-minute Rule reminds you that if a task takes less than 2-minutes, do it right now. This way you prevent small tasks from piling up unnecessarily. Example – organizing a folder on your laptop, replying to an email or putting dishes in the dishwasher.

ACTIVITY:

Apply the Two-Minute Rule

Think of any tasks you can apply the two-minute rule to, and practice it.

1.
2.
3.
4.
5.

During my work with Sheena, she learnt the above techniques and applied them in her daily life. She left out things that were taking away her time (scrolling on Instagram) and used the matrix to prioritize tasks that needed to be done that day so that if she didn't get to the other tasks, she could still leave work on time. She used the Pomodoro technique to be more focused and less distracted as she worked on her marketing task. Utilizing these techniques helped her free up her time earlier in the day to be able to attend her salsa class at 5:30pm instead of 7:30pm. By managing her time better, Sheena was able to get all her work done in time by 5pm and get into bed by 10pm ensuring she was able to find balance in her daily life.

Time management does not mean having a rigid schedule, it means finding a balance that works the best for you. Create your daily, weekly, and monthly goals while using the techniques mentioned above to create a realistic and achievable time management plan for yourself.

Reviewing and Reflecting

Congratulations for reaching this point! You're halfway in! I am so excited and proud of you for coming this far. Phew, two weeks have gone by. Often when we are working towards our goals, we make the mistake of wrapping up goal 1, onto goal 2, and so on, never stopping to take a breath, to acknowledge, celebrate or tweak that goal. But here, you are not going to make that mistake.

So, before you move on to the next two weeks, I want you to look at the progress you have made, assess the hurdles that came up, see if you need to change any goals, or maybe just celebrate your wins so far. Reviewing and reflecting will give you the opportunity to look back at what's been working, what's not, and how your behaviors have been aligning with your goals. Today is divided into three sections to assess all the work you have done so far. Let's go for it.

Section 1:
Review Your Goals

In the first 4 days, you identified a life domain you had concerns in, made SMART goals to work on those concerns, and made sure those goals were aligned with your core values while mapping your goals via milestones. You are now going to revisit those goals and assess your progress to check if you're on track or there is a need to adjust your focus.

ACTIVITY:
Assess Your Goals

In the template below, write down your life domain, area of concern(s), and goal(s) from Days 1 and 2, and the corresponding aligned value from Day 3. Re-reading your goals, check if they still resonate with you. In order to track your progress, ask yourself the following questions:

- What steps have I taken towards reaching this goal?

- Did I achieve my milestones? (Check your worksheets from Day 4)

- Did I face any obstacles? (Day 4)

- Did my proposed solutions work, or do I need to find alternative solutions? (Day 4)

- Where am I on my path to achieving this goal? Rate it on a scale of 1 (no progress) to 10 (goal achieved).

- If you want to make any adjustments to your goal, what is your new goal?

Example:

Life Domain: Physical Health

Area of Concern: I am not healthy.

Goal: Exercise for 30 minutes 5 days a week

Aligned Value: Fitness

Steps Taken: I took a gym membership and have been exercising 3 days a week, 45 min each.

Milestones achieved: identified available options, tried different things, joined the gym, started exercising regularly.

Obstacles Faced: Lack of motivation

Solutions: I proposed wanting a gym buddy that didn't work out, feasibility-wise but I was able to ask a friend to keep me accountable by checking up on me, which worked.

Progress Score: 7

Goal Adjustment: Exercising 4 days a week, instead of 5 because that would work better with my schedule and time available, instead of wanting to do it 5 days, not being able to and then feeling guilty about it.

Go ahead and fill the template to check progress on your goals.

Goal 1

Life Domain: _____

Area of Concern: _____

Goal: _____

Aligned Value: _____

Steps Taken: _____

Milestones achieved: _____

Obstacles Faced: _____

Solutions: _____

Progress Score: _____

Goal Adjustment: _____

Goal 2

Life Domain: _____

Area of Concern: _____

Goal: _____

Aligned Value: _____

Steps Taken: _____

Milestones achieved: _____

Obstacles Faced: _____

Solutions: _____

Progress Score: _____

Goal Adjustment: _____

Having done that, make sure to acknowledge and appreciate how far you have come, notice the progress you have made and the challenges you have overcome to reach here. Take a moment to celebrate your success so far, however, seemingly minimal. We do have the tendency to minimize our achievements and maximize our 'failures' (a cognitive distortion called magnification) and I don't want you to make that thinking error.

Section 2:
Reflect on How You Think

On days 5 to 8, you learnt how thoughts impact your feelings and behaviors, began to identify errors you were making in your thinking, and noticed your thought patterns before challenging them. On days 9 and 10, you learnt to positively reframe some of these negative thought patterns and to test them out using a behavioral experiment.

You will now be reflecting on any changes that might have happened in the way you think (especially relating to the cognitive distortions) in the last few days. Once you have acknowledged the progress you have made so far, you will be committing to the next steps, continuing your journey to constructive thinking. It is important to recognize any mental shifts to be able to gauge your progress and then continue to work on it for lasting long-term change.

ACTIVITY:
Reviewing Mindshift Change

Write down in the table below, cognitive distortions you noticed yourself engaging in (Day 6 and 7). Do you notice any changes in these patterns of thinking? Which cognitive distortions are you still working to change? Choose one or two distortions to actively work on for next week. Use CRAFTED to challenge them (Day 8) and positively reframe these thoughts (Day 9). *Here's an example:*

Cognitive Distortion(s) identified	Progress Made/ New Thought	Working on (Cognitive Distortion)	Reframed thought
Magnification ("I cannot do anything right") Catastrophizing	"I am trying my best, it's okay to make mistakes sometimes, I am only human."	Catastrophizing ("I am going to mess up my upcoming presentation and I will never be given another chance again.")	"I am going to give it my best and if something goes wrong, I am capable of dealing with it."

Now try it here:

Cognitive Distortion(s) identified	Progress Made/ New Thought	Working on (Cognitive Distortion)	Reframed thought

Remember, you have had a long time using a certain mindset so be patient and kind to yourself if it's seemingly taking you longer to change it. You have started on the process and that's a great thing. Changing your mindset is a much longer process and the key is to keep at it and not give up. Once again, make sure to applaud yourself for the progress made so far before continuing on your mindshift journey.

Section 3:
Reviewing Behavioral Progress

On days 11 to 14, you worked directly on your behaviors. You identified avoidance behaviors, pushed yourself to take actions, engaged in enjoyable activities, and built healthy habits. Now it's time to analyze these behavioral changes, reinforce positive habits, and bring change where improvements are required.

ACTIVITY:
Behavioral Reflection

Looking back over the last few days, identify any new habits or behaviors you have developed. Have you been eating right, making time for self-care, or meeting friends regularly? Identify what behaviors you are engaging in that are helping you reach closer to your goals. Having done that, think about which areas still need to improve, what do you want to focus on now. Make an action plan to work on your continued progress. Use the below table to review the process so far and plan for the next steps.

New Behaviors	Areas to improve on	Action Plans
Not procrastinating work by watching TV instead	Manage stress when deadlines are coming up	• Take deep breaths when stressing out • Get up and take a short walk when it's getting too much
Established a night slow-down, self-care routine before bed	Not sleeping on time which makes me feel tired in the mornings and sets me off for the entire day	• Set reminders to get into bed at a certain time • Put my phone away before getting into bed

Try it here:

New Behaviors	Areas to improve on	Action Plans

You took out time today to reflect and review the last two weeks. In the process, you paused, acknowledged, and celebrated your wins so far, before identifying possible obstacles and how to work around them for the next two weeks. Well done! CBT helps you understand yourself on a deeper level and to align your goals and behaviors to get to being the person you want to be and achieve your goals. You have set the foundation; you have learnt a lot about yourself, and you are working every day to get to the best version of yourself. I am proud of you, and you should be proud of yourself.

PART 4

Managing Anxiety and Fear

In the last 15 days, you have learnt a lot about the way you think, feel, and behave. So far, I have stuck to common everyday situations to help you identify and recognize your own patterns. Now that you are more aware of your thoughts, feelings, and behaviors, let us focus on some specific feelings. During the next 3 days, I will be focusing on the feelings of anxiety and fear to help you understand how these feelings show up for you, what are some of the situations that trigger these feelings and the best way to manage them.

On day 16, you will be understanding the nature of anxiety, what it is, and in which ways it shows up. Understanding the concept of anxiety in general will give you clarity about the purpose anxiety has been serving in your life. You will be able to identify triggers of anxiety and fear in your daily life situations. Finally, you will introspect on how anxiety shows up for you, its cognitive, behavioral, and physiological symptoms.

Day 17 will help you learn techniques to manage your anxiety and fears. Using the principles of breathing and mindfulness, you will learn to control the effects of anxiety in your physical body. These will, in turn, affect your anxious thoughts and behaviors. On day 18, you will learn to face your anxiety and fears. Avoidance is often seen in the face of fear. Sometimes, the anxiety is overwhelming, and you decide not to take that exam or that interview. You will learn how to face your fears in a step-by-step manner using graded exposure techniques. By the end of this section, you will better understand your feelings of anxiety and fear, learn how to tackle and face them without being overwhelmed.

DAY 16:

Understanding Anxiety and Fear

Anxiety and fear are emotions that we all experience from time to time. Both these emotions have a very adaptive function. Back in the prehistoric times, anxiety and fear were adaptive ways of keeping us safe from threat and danger like wild animals or fire. Now that we live comparatively non-dangerous daily lives (cities instead of forests, etc.), anxiety comes up in different ways.

The function of these emotions is still to protect us and keep us safe. These are not negative emotions in general. What makes them negative is the situations they come up in (in case of non-threatening situations), the intensity with which they come up (if not proportionate to the situation), the duration they last, and the effect they have on our behaviors (prevent us from being our best versions by becoming roadblocks).

Anxiety often emanates from the anticipation of things occurring in the future[8]. For example, some of your anxiety might be stemming from how you will manage to finish all your work goals before your upcoming trip next week. Anxiety is the body and mind's way of preparing you for the worst possible outcome like it did for the archaic homo sapiens to protect them from being eaten by predatory animals. The function of anxiety is adaptive but the situation it is showing up in or the way it shows up might be harmful instead of being helpful. For example, anxiety motivates you to finish your work before the deadline but if present at a severe intensity, it will make it harder for you to focus and prevent you from meeting your goals.

Fear, on the other hand, is a more immediate response to a threat or danger. It manifests itself in one of the three ways: flight (you run away from a rat in the room), fight (you pick up a broom to hit the rat with), or freeze (fear paralyzes and roots you to one spot, you may or may not be able to scream for help)[9]. Newer investigations have reported other reactions like faint (at the sight of the rat), fool (imitating the voice of cat to fool the rat into running away), pray, or fawn (trying to remain in the room even when uncomfortable and anxious)[10].

Fear, again, is the body's response to alert you to danger to take immediate action. Compared to anxiety, fear is usually short-lived, and the impact reduces when the immediate threat is taken away. You might continue to fear rats, but the actual fear reaction would not present itself if there was no danger of the presence of a rat. In order to better understand the difference between fear and anxiety, think of it in this manner. Fear is about what is happening right now, in this very moment while anxiety is more about what is going to happen in the future.

How Anxiety and Fear Show Up

Anxiety and fear show up in your thoughts, feelings, body, and behaviors. Physical symptoms of anxiety and fear look like:

- Shortness of breath

- Increased heart rate

- Dry mouth

- Sweating

- Dizziness

- Nausea

- Stomach ache or discomfort

In the previous days, we have talked about thoughts that are related to anxiety. These automatic negative thoughts are often preceded by 'what if', in anticipation of the anxiety-provoking situation(s). "What if I fail?" "What if he breaks up with me?" "If I don't get this job, my life will be ruined." Can you recognize some of the cognitive distortions in these thoughts? Thinking errors often result in anxiety.

During fear, the focus is on the danger situation and immediate protection. Thoughts at this time are about how to protect oneself. You could also engage in cognitive distortions during this time like, "What if this dog bit me and I died of the bite (catastrophizing/ magnification)?" In terms of behavior, anxiety shows up in -

Behavior	Actions	Examples
Avoidance Behaviors	Avoiding any anxiety-provoking situation	I am going to take a sick leave today because I am too scared of the meeting today and what will happen during it.
Safety Behaviors	Taking actions to reduce what one perceives as risky situations	Constantly checking your emails to be able to quickly see any email from your boss and respond quickly – "If I am not quick enough in my responses to him, he might think I don't work hard and may fire me."
Procrastination	Putting off tasks based on fear of failure or judgment	Not sending the draft to your boss because you want it to be perfect first.

As you can notice from the above examples, both avoidance and safety behaviors will actually reinforce your anxiety so even though they provide relief in the short-term, over the long-term, they maintain your anxiety.

As previously mentioned, fear shows up in -

- Fight – Raising your voice, getting tensed
- Flight – Avoiding confrontation or conflicts
- Freeze – Unable to act due to overwhelming fear, loss of voice
- Faint – physical reaction when fear becomes unbearable
- Fool – attempt to get out of the situation
- Pray – hoping someone will save you from the fearful situation
- Fawn – appease the threat

The Anxiety Cycle

Another important thing to understand is that anxiety operates in a cyclical pattern. Once it shows up, it inserts itself into a loop of worry and avoidance. It is crucial to identify this cycle in order to break it. A usual pattern looks like this-

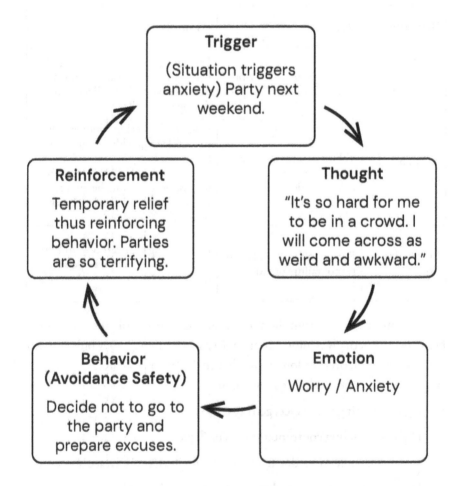

Now that you have a better understanding of the nature of anxiety and fear and how they manifest, it is time to recognize these emotions in your life and how they show up for you.

ACTIVITY:

Recognizing Your Anxiety and Fear

Triggers:

Identify your triggers. What situations cause you to be anxious or fearful? Is it work meetings, crowded events, or getting into an elevator? How does anxiety or fear show up for you in terms of physical symptoms, thoughts, and behaviors?

Physical symptoms: _____

Thoughts: _____

Behaviors: _____

How do you respond to fearful situations?

- Fight
- Flight
- Freeze
- Faint
- Fool
- Pray
- Fawn

You may be engaging in one or more of the above behaviors, depending on the situation. Write down which responses typically show up in which situations.

Example:

☐ Fight   ☑ Flight   ☐ Freeze   ☐ Faint

☐ Fool   ☐ Fawn   ☐ Pray

Flight comes up when the danger seems too big to handle. Like

when I feel a stranger may be following me.

_____

_____

☐ Fight   ☐ Flight   ☐ Freeze   ☐ Faint

☐ Fool   ☐ Fawn   ☐ Pray

_____

_____

_____

Now identify your anxiety cycle.

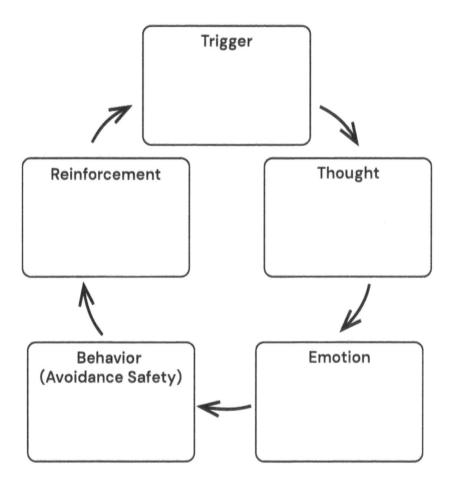

By getting an in-depth understanding of the feelings of anxiety and fear and how they look in your life, you are getting ready to work on managing them. Remember, anxiety and fear are normal emotions, and it is okay to experience them in our daily life. The only time we need to worry about them is when they cause distress (incapacitating amounts of anxiety or fear) or dysfunction (cause hurdles in your work/personal/social life). Tomorrow, we will work on managing these situations where anxiety or fear become overwhelming.

Learning Techniques to Manage Anxiety and Fear

Armed with a better understanding of how feelings of anxiety and fear show up in your life, you are now ready to deal with these emotions. As a reminder, we are not aiming at entirely removing these feelings. These are necessary emotions that protect us from danger. My attempt today is to help you learn to manage these feelings when they occur in seemingly innocuous situations or when your reactions are disproportionate to the amount of danger these situations pose in reality. I will be teaching you three techniques to calm yourself down, reduce your physical reactions in the face of anxiety and fear, and to be able to think clearly by bringing yourself back to the present moment.

Box Breathing

One of the common physical symptoms of anxiety and fear is our heart rate rises, and our breath becomes shallow, heightening the feeling of anxiety making it harder to relax. A shallow, heightened pace of breathing fuels the fight or flight response in your body by activating the sympathetic nervous system. Breathing deeply activates your parasympathetic system, which is active during moments of rest and relaxation.[11]

Here are the steps to Box Breathing:

1. Sit in a comfortable position in a place with minimal distractions,

2. Place one hand on your abdomen,

3. Inhale slowly and deeply through your nose for a count of 4, feel your stomach being inflated,

4. Hold your breath for a count of 4,

5. Exhale slowly and gradually through your mouth for a count of 4, noticing your stomach deflating,

6. Hold your breath for a count of 4,

7. Repeat for 5-10 minutes as desired.

Box breathing reduces your feelings of anxiety, calms you down, and thereby clears up your thought process to help you make the right choice and not out of anxiety or fear.

ACTIVITY:
Practice Box Breathing

Practice Box breathing now for 5 minutes. Once you finish, reflect on how you feel in your body and mind. Depending on the situation, you can practice box breathing anywhere. Once you practice it enough in neutral situations, you can even do it during your commute when you don't need to keep the hand on your stomach to notice you are breathing deep into your stomach. The idea is to practice it enough in your daily life to be able to utilize it during anxiety or fear-provoking situations.

Mindfulness

Remember I told you anxiety is often rooted into the future based on our past experiences? Based on this logic, it will be helpful to bring you back from the past and future (thoughts) into the present. That is exactly what mindfulness does. Mindfulness is staying in the present moment. It is about being in the 'here and now.' When you focus on what is happening right now, you can look away from what has happened in the past or what will happen in the future. Mindfulness has time and again proved to be beneficial for managing anxiety.[12] In CBT, mindfulness ensures being present in the moment and accepting experiences, whether good or bad. This helps you break free from negative thought cycles, pertaining to the past or future, thereby, leading to adaptive emotional regulation.

Mindfulness can be practiced in many ways. You can meditate mindfully, walk mindfully, even eat or drink mindfully. The key is to be fully present. A thing to keep in mind is to approach this as a first step. You don't run a marathon on your first run. You start with 1km, 2km, 5km and so on. You build your stamina, and you practice over and over again until your body is physically ready. The same is true for your mind. If you have never practiced being mindful before, do not expect it to happen in your first attempt. Your mind will go back to its comfort zone, worrying about things to come, planning your day, or even thinking how this is a waste of time. And that is okay. You are only going to gently nudge your mind to come back to the present moment, over and over again. Every day, every week, every month, until it comes more naturally. Be patient, your mind is learning something new, give it time.

ACTIVITY:
Mindful Drinking

Let's start small and practice mindful drinking. What do you drink daily? Coffee, tea, lemonade, a protein shake? Whatever it is. Bring it and get ready. Now you are going to indulge all your senses.

- What do you see? What color is your drink? How thick or viscous does it look? What glass or tumbler is it in? Does the color seem appealing?

- What do you smell? Take a whiff. What does your drink smell like? Is it the fragrance of coffee, ginger, lemon, or chocolate?

- What do you touch? Is the mug warm or cold to touch? Is it hot or merely warm? Is it cold or icy?

- What do you hear? Give your drink a light swirl. Did you hear that swish? Blowing off the hot drink, did that make a sound? Does your slurping make any sound?

- What do you taste? Take a sip. What does that taste like? The bitterness of coffee, the tang of lime, or the taste of chocolate?

- What do you feel? Do you feel the liquid going down your throat? How does that feel on your tongue, in your throat?

Try to notice as many details as possible, there is no rush. Take it slow. How do you feel after this activity? How was your focus during the activity? Did your mind want to rush to something else? That is normal for the first time. Were you able to bring back your attention once it drifted? That is what you want to try doing every time you are distracted. Can you try and practice mindful drinking at least once during your day to practice being mindful? Later, you can also choose to walk mindfully, eat mindfully, or do any other activity in your day with your focus on the present moment.

Mindfulness: Grounding

The final technique that I want to teach you today is very helpful in situations which are high-strung and your anxiety or fear is going through the roof. This hardly takes 5 minutes, but it helps you bring your attention back to the present. Grounding helps you reorient yourself, thereby reducing the feelings of anxiety and fear. Here are the steps to a grounding exercise especially when feeling anxious, try to:

1. **Look around you.** Name (out loud or silently in your mind) 5 things you see around you. Notice the colors, shapes, and textures of these things, think about their uses.

2. **Feel.** What are the 4 things you can feel? Maybe the bed underneath you or the clothes on your skin, the cushion against your back, the phone in your hand. How do they feel? Rough, soft, hard, grainy, cold, warm?

3. **Hear.** What 3 things can you hear? People talking, music, the fan, your breathing, a bird? How quiet or loud is the sound? Is it a usual or infrequent sound? Is it pleasant or unpleasant to your ears?

4. **Smell.** What 2 things can you smell? Your perfume, room fragrance, the incense you burn in the morning, your shampoo? Do you like or dislike the smell? Do you smell it often or infrequently? What does it smell like-can you identify the tones?

5. **Taste.** What is the one thing you can taste? Is it the aftertaste of the toothpaste or the lingering taste of chocolate in your mouth? Do you like the taste? If you can't taste anything, go find something to taste whose flavor you like.

Grounding practice is very useful when you feel overwhelmed and on edge. It helps slow you down, helping you get clarity of thought to make the best decisions for yourself instead of engaging in avoidance or safety behaviors which come naturally with anxious thoughts.

ACTIVITY:
Grounding Practice

Practice grounding activity to get a feel for it. After the exercise, notice how you are feeling. The techniques you learned today might seem simple, but they are great to reduce the way your body reacts to anxious situations. By engaging in any of the above techniques, you are reducing the physical symptoms I talked about yesterday. When physical symptoms of anxiety and fear are reduced, you are able to think about it differently (cognitive symptoms), thereby impacting your behavioral symptoms and hence breaking the cycle of anxiety.

Having said that, these simple exercises will not come naturally to you during moments of anxiety and fear unless you practice them in neutral situations on a regular basis. Take out 10 minutes daily to practice these 3 techniques. Use them to relax after a long, stressful day or to prepare yourself before an intense meeting at work. Tomorrow you will learn how to manage your fears.

DAY 18:

Facing Your Anxiety and Fear

Yesterday, you learnt techniques to manage your anxiety and fears. These techniques were aimed at reducing the feelings of anxiety and fear, and managing them better. Today, we will learn about how to face these overwhelming situations and to change our behaviors surrounding these anxieties and fears.

On day 16, we learned that anxiety leads us to avoidance, safety, and procrastination behaviors which, in turn, continue the anxiety cycle and keep the loop going. Fear, on the other hand, leads to fight, flight, freeze, fool, and pray behaviors. Towards the end of day 16, you recognized your anxiety cycle and your typical behaviors in a fearful situation. Today, we are going to face your anxieties and fears utilizing a process called graded exposure.

Exposure means facing your fears, confronting them head-on. The addition of the word 'graded' means we are going to do it in small, incremental steps. The day before, you had become aware of how avoiding anxiety-provoking situations only keeps the loop going, catching you in a vicious anxiety cycle. In order to work on anxiety in the long-term, you need to get out of that cycle by altering your behaviors. When you face your fears in a controlled and safe environment as a behavioral experiment, the fear and anxieties reduce, and you can reclaim control of your life.

Graded exposure allows you to take small but significant steps towards eliminating your fears by facing them. When done in an incremental and sequential manner, the process feels less stressful and more empowering. Imagine a ladder, it is easier to climb, step by step. The more steps you skip, the harder it becomes to climb. Graded exposure, a behavioral component of CBT, has been very effective in reducing anxiety and fears, with virtual reality exposure now being used in therapy[13]. Here are the steps for graded exposure:

1. What are your fears? Write down the situations or things that are fearful for you. Rank these fears on a scale from 1-least fearful to 10-most fearful.

2. Pick a fear that is on the lowest score.

3. For this fear, identify different situations in which it comes up. Create a hierarchy of these situations based on the above scale (1-least fearful to 10-most fearful). Add as many situations as possible.

4. Set realistic goals of where you can start from. 1 might be too easy and 10 would overwhelm you. Find something that causes mild to moderate fear or anxiety and begin there.

5. Gradually expose yourself to the lowest anxiety-provoking situation. Repeat the exposure to this situation as many times as needed. Move up the hierarchy only when the anxiety or fear on the current step becomes mild.

6. Maintain a record to track your progress.

Ben had a disabling fear of social situations. It was hard for him to go to the bank or even a grocery store. He hardly left his home, had a remote job, and got all his groceries delivered at home. Even a video call was anxiety provoking for him. This was adversely impacting his personal life, none of his relationships continued past the one-month mark. He had no social life. Professionally, he had to rely on remote jobs that only required interacting with a computer, he was not able to attend video calls or meetings or network with colleagues. Ben approached me online via an email. Realizing his fear of video calls, we stuck to emails and messaging to begin with.

Graded exposure steps with Ben looked like:

1.

Fear	Rank
Getting stuck in an elevator	9
Fear of social situations	8
Fear of dogs	7

2. Even though his fear of dogs was the lowest number, his fear of going outside in the presence of several others, would make it hard for him to be exposed to dogs, so we decided to tackle his fear of social situations first.

3.

Fear comes up in situations of	Rank
Going to the grocery store	9
Going to the park	6
Going to the bank	7
Meeting colleagues	10
Video call with someone	5

4. We identified being on a video call was the least fearful for him. But I wanted him to further divide it into different situations to start from an even lower score.

   - Video call with stranger – 5
   - Video call with friend – 4
   - Video call with Mom – 3

5. We decided from the lowest score of 3. The activity was for him to get on a video call with his mom. As expected, he was resistant because even thinking about it brought up a lot of anxiety for him. I reminded him of skills he had learnt to work on his anxiety. (You have also learnt techniques to manage your anxiety yesterday. Put them to good use.) It was a video call with his mom, he had access to techniques to reduce his anxiety, he had control of the situation and could disconnect the call if he felt it was becoming too much. We established the experiment as – Preparing for the call, 5 minutes box breathing, making the call, 5 minutes box breathing/ grounding exercise.

6. Ben reported how it went for him. He reported being anxious, but the box breathing helped. The first few minutes were scary but later, he relaxed and by the time he disconnected the call after 10 minutes, he was feeling calmer than he previously would have. We then started working on making a video call with a friend.

Over 3 weeks of emails later, Ben was ready to engage in a video call with a stranger. This is how we started having video call sessions and then worked on the rest of Ben's hierarchy list. It took several months for Ben to work on his severe social anxiety. Now, Ben is in an eight-month-long relationship, goes for a daily walk to the park, buys his own groceries from the store, and is able to go to the bank. He still holds a remote job because he prefers it, but he can now get on video calls and even goes to the office for social networking meetups. Now that you have a better idea of the process, follow these steps for yourself.

ACTIVITY:
Graded Exposure

1. What are your fears and anxieties? Rank them.

Fear	Rank

2. Identify different situations in which the fear with the lowest score comes up.

Fear comes up in situations of	Rank

3. Set realistic goals of where you can start from. Find something that causes mild to moderate fear or anxiety and begin there.

_____

_____

4. Gradually expose yourself to the situation. Move up the hierarchy when the anxiety or fear on the current step becomes mild.

_____

_____

5. Maintain a record to track your progress.

_____

_____

A couple of things to remember during this process.

*   Be patient and kind with yourself. These fears have been a part of your life for far too long. They cannot be overcome in a day. Go slow. Give yourself enough time.

*   Be consistent. You might have to repeat exposure to a single situation 10 times before you feel you are ready to go to the next step. Do not give up. Do the exposure as often as you can.

*   Do not rush. Do not move too fast. If you do that, you might risk giving up. Take your time with each step, as long as you need.

You are now equipped to work on your physical symptoms of anxiety and fears (day 17). Today, you have been changing your behaviors to face your fears and anxieties instead of avoiding them (day 18). Tomorrow, we will be working on your thoughts and carrying over from part 2 of the workbook.

PART 5

Challenging Core Beliefs and Fostering a Positive Mindset

Now that you are well-equipped to manage your anxiety and fears, this section will focus on bringing a deeper shift in your core beliefs, teach you how to apply the techniques you already learnt to other domains of your life, and help you develop a positive mindset.

Day 19 will give you a deeper insight into why you think the way you think. You will understand the origin of your deep-rooted beliefs and where they stem from. This awareness will help you see the error you are making by continuing to hold onto this belief. Utilizing the techniques previously learnt, you will challenge these beliefs and reframe them to witness a longer lasting change.

On Day 20, you will learn the concept of neuroplasticity and how it relates to rewiring your brain from negativity to positivity. You will learn to write new scripts for your distressing memories, and shift your mindset. You will be visualizing a future version of yourself that you aspire to so that you can continue to work towards it.

Day 21 is to review and reflect on your journey so far. You will be taking a look at your initial goals, tracking your progress, and making adjustments as needed. You will reflect on how you are managing your anxiety and fear, and to identify what techniques work the best for you. You will check your progress on action plans made to reframe your negative core beliefs. Finally, you will revisit and reflect on your growth mindset.

By the end of this section, you will gain deeper insights into your core beliefs and how it impacts your anxiety, fear, and low self-esteem. You will learn to keep a balanced and positive mindset.

Working on Deep-Rooted Beliefs

In the last few days, you have worked on managing your physical sensations and reducing your avoidance behaviors in order to tackle anxiety. Today, we will be working on your thoughts. We have done some work on your thoughts in part 2 of this workbook. I will be building on that today. Earlier in this workbook, you learnt that it is your thoughts about the situation, rather than the situation itself, which affects your feelings. These feelings then lead to certain physical sensations (like increased heart rate when feeling anxious). And these physical sensations then determine your behavior.

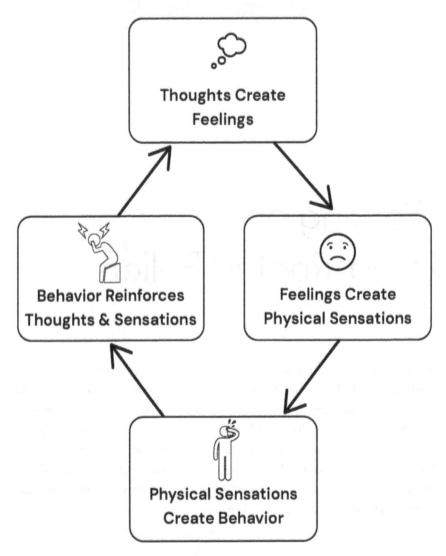

Today, we will be going back to Day 1 of this workbook where you identified the root causes behind your concerns. Now you are at a better place to do a deep dive into some of those. Take a look at your last worksheet from Day 1, what were the root causes you identified. For the example I gave, 'fear of rejection' came up as a root cause of the concerns being faced in the relationship domain.

In this instance, fear of rejection is not merely a cognitive distortion but a schema. A schema is a deep-rooted way of thinking or feeling that affects how you interpret situations. They are deep rooted because they often find origin in childhood experiences and have had enough time to develop long and strong roots. Imagine a tree that has been planted 20 years ago. It's very hard to up-root it because its roots are far-reaching as compared to a plant which has been recently planted. These schemas are the root causes of a number of issues like anxiety, self-esteem, and even cause relationship conflicts.

Today, you are going to understand the nature of these schemas, become better at identifying them, and then learn how to manage these core beliefs so that you can uproot them and stop them from affecting the areas of your life. Negative schemas, the ones we need to work on, distort the way you look at things or perceive a given situation. These schemas are your thoughts about yourself, your future, and the world[14].

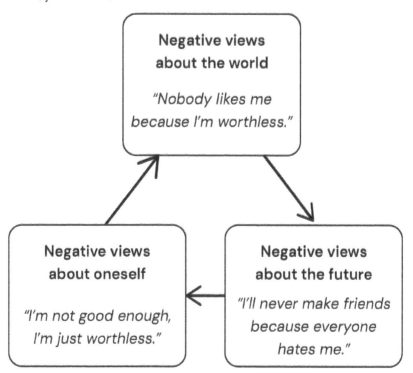

Some examples of negative schemas are-

- No one loves me.
- I am a failure.
- I don't deserve to be loved.
- I am worthless.
- Everyone leaves me.

It's important to understand how schemas develop. They are formed during childhood based on your experiences. What happens in your early relationships (with parents, primary caregivers, siblings, or friends), your early experiences (bullying, abuse, trauma), and your early environments (conflicts between parents, immigration, living in a war zone) decides your schemas. It does not mean that every individual in similar circumstances would develop the exact same schemas. It depends on a lot of other factors like your temperament, personality, protective, and mediating factors. I will not go into detail because it is outside the scope of this workbook.

Let us take the example of Dan. As a child, he faced a lot of criticism growing up because his parents wanted him to be the best version of himself. They wanted to push him to win in each area of his life, be it academics, sports, or extracurricular activities. But in doing so, they would make remarks like, 'Oh, Dan. What happened? You know you have it in you to be the best. Why were you placed second? That's not good enough', or 'It's disappointing that the other guy did better in basketball than you. You have got two inches on him!' To Dan, it felt like no matter how hard he tried, it was never good enough. He was never good enough.

As he grew older, circumstances changed but this deep-rooted core belief or schema was resistant to change. Dan was never able to celebrate a win because he didn't think he was good enough. He was always disappointed in himself and had low self-esteem. He could never take compliments from his manager as he felt he didn't deserve them. This had an effect on how his manager thought about him and he never got the promotion he worked hard for and deserved because that is the kind of image he projected as a result of his low self-esteem. And because he was never promoted, it reinforced Dan's belief in his limited abilities.

Does this help you understand how something that developed in childhood, and persisted through adulthood, can impact your life in such adverse ways? But why do we still carry these childhood thoughts? Because time and again, these negative schemas have been confirmed by life experiences, keeping them intact, as demonstrated in the example above. Someone who has a fear of rejection will avoid making close friendships which will, in turn, reinforce the belief that others will reject them. Letting go of these schemas involves a deeper awareness of them before you can challenge them.

ACTIVITY:
Identify Your Schemas

Let's identify your schemas. You might have unraveled some in the Day 1 worksheet. To find others, ask yourself these questions-

- What beliefs I hold about myself that may be affecting my anxiety and self-esteem?

- How do I look at my relationships, my work performance, and my success?

Some possible themes that may come up are 'I will always fail.' 'No matter what I do, things will always go wrong,' or 'Everyone will leave me.'

Write down your schemas in the following template.

Now, think back to your childhood and try to identify the origin of these schemas. How was the communication with your parents or primary caregivers? How did you feel during your childhood? How was your time in school, did you get along with your peers? Were there any adverse circumstances in your household or city while you were growing up?

Write down your observations about the origin of your schemas.

The next step is to recognize what triggers these schemas for you. Do they come up in certain situations or with specific people? This recognition will help you prepare well in advance and be mindful of these triggers. Write down your triggers corresponding to each schema. *Here's an example:*

Schema	Origin	Trigger
I am worthless.	Growing up, my father would always berate me and was never happy with anything I did. He would always find faults in my behaviors. It was like nothing I could do was ever right. He used to tell me often, 'you are good for nothing'.	It often comes up with authority figures like my parents, my manager, my in-laws, or the priest at my Church.

Now try this for yourself below-

Schema	Origin	Trigger

Schema	Origin	Trigger

ACTIVITY:
Challenging Schemas

You will now be utilizing and revising some of your learning from Days 8, 9, and 10. In order to challenge these schemas, ask yourself the following questions-

- Is this always true, or may there be exceptions?
- Is this the reality or am I interpreting the situation based on my perspective?
- Do I have any evidence contrary to my belief?

You can use the CRAFTED technique you learnt on Day 8 and apply it to your schemas.

Example:

For a schema of 'fear of rejection', you would be looking at exception-situations where your friends might love you and not reject you, but you seem to be focusing only on situations or people who reject you. On day 9, you learnt to positively reframe your distortion, do that for your schema now. For the schema of 'fear of rejection,' reframing will look like, 'There are people who love me for who I am.'

On Day 10, you learnt to test out your thoughts using behavioral experiments. Carry out one for your schema now. Make an action plan for the same. For your 'fear of rejection', try putting yourself in mildly anxiety-provoking situations where you fear rejection to see if your belief is really true. Remember Leah who asked a stranger for directions? *Here's an example:*

Schema	Challenge	Reframe	Action Plan
I am worthless.	Not everyone thinks I am worthless. My friends and my partner appreciate what I do for them. My manager has praised me in the past.	Sometimes some people may criticize me, but there are others who see my worth and appreciate me for who I am.	At work tomorrow, I will notice after day end, if there were things I did that were important to the organization. I will ask my close friend in what way am I bringing value to her life.

Now, try this for one of your schemas.

Schema	Challenge	Reframe	Action Plan

Keep in mind the difference between a thought and a schema is the extent to which it is embedded, and the amount of time needed to restructure and change it. Even though the process looks similar, you will have to spend more time introspecting on the origin of the schema and then to challenge and restructure it multiple times to see any improvement. Be patient with yourself and the process. By working on dismantling negative schemas, you are removing the thoughts that lead to feelings of anxiety, thereby, finding a solution to your anxiety at its very source. Make sure you do the exercises you learnt today on a regular and consistent basis as schemas are resistant to change and need to be chipped away, a bit at a time.

Rewiring Your Brain from Negativity to Positivity

In the last 20 days, you have spent a lot of time looking at your thoughts, analyzing and reframing them to have the best impact on your feelings and behaviors. Today, you will focus on consciously developing positive thinking patterns to aid the process of reframing that you have already put into action.

With the practice of positive thinking, you will be empowered to have a more optimistic approach to life. Often when we engage in cognitive distortions like magnification or discounting the positive, we unconsciously choose to focus on the negative while not looking at the positives in the situation. Positive thinking asks us to make a conscious effort to look for and acknowledge the positives.

Positive thinking does not mean you are living in denial or not looking at the reality. It is more about having a balanced outlook. It is about interpreting situations in a manner which empowers you to take action instead of making you fearful, thereby, preventing you from taking action.

Positive thinking helps in manifold ways-

- **Mental Health.** Thinking positively alleviates symptoms of anxiety and depression.

- **Self-Esteem.** Focusing on your strengths and abilities helps you feel good about yourself instead of thinking only about your weaknesses.

- **Interpersonal Relationships.** Everyone likes an optimistic person. If you are always in a negative mindset, you will push away people.

Today, you will learn how to harness the natural ability of your brain to rewire itself, a process known as neuroplasticity. Neuroplasticity is the capacity of your brain to adapt and re-learn based on your experiences, thoughts, and behaviors. Every time you think in a certain way, your brain strengthens these thought patterns. As time passes, these patterns then become habits. So, the more you think negatively, those patterns are solidified. On the other hand, if you think positively, your brain will learn these healthier ways of thinking.[15]

Think of it like going to the gym where you build body muscles. Through neuroplasticity, you are developing brain muscles. The more you use these muscles, the stronger they become. The choice is yours; do you want to strengthen negative or positive thinking? As you focus on rewiring your brain from negativity to positivity today, you are literally changing the structure of your brain! How amazing is that?

Take the case of Lilah. Lilah was always the glass half empty kind of a person. She was always critical about people and situations. She used to complain about anything and everything. To the extent that her friends started avoiding her because it seemed like she brought so much negativity with her that by the time they left the gathering, they would all be feeling miserable. Lilah would complain about the weather, gossip negatively about her colleagues, it seemed like she never had a good thing to say about anyone. No one liked her at work because they felt if she was talking critically about one colleague, she might be doing the same for them. As a result, she lost her relationships with her friends and colleagues and rarely could hold onto a longer-term personal relationship.

When Lilah came to me, she said, "No one understands me. I don't get why they ignore me. I am such a nice person and always willing to help. No one seems to appreciate what I bring to the table." It was only by our fourth session together that I could understand what was going wrong.

During all our time together, Lilah used to complain about everything. If it was sunny, she complained about getting freckles; if it was raining, she worried her hair would be ruined; if it was windy, she felt no one would be able to see the new dress she was wearing under the coat. You get the idea. It took me several more sessions to help reflect this to Lilah in a manner which she could understand. And once she became aware of what was happening, we were then able to work on fostering a positive mindset and being more mindful of what she communicated in her interactions. Here are some of the things we worked on in our time together to harness the power of neuroplasticity for Lilah.

Rescripting using Imagery

This CBT tool helps you reprocess and reframe distressing memories in a positive manner, particularly those rooted in negative core schemas. This powerful neuroplasticity exercise helps you change the way you think about past events and reframe them in a more positive light. Remember, this is not about rewriting history but about creating a different narrative that empowers you instead of you avoiding certain behaviors. This effective therapeutic technique has been proven beneficial for people with anxiety, depression and those who have experienced trauma.[16] Here's how to go about it.

1. **Identify a distressing (not traumatic) memory.** A traumatic memory can be deeply distressing and can elicit overwhelming emotions which would be difficult to process by yourself. In order to work with a traumatic memory, you should do so in the presence or guidance of a mental health professional. For this exercise, choose a memory that's distressing but manageable. Pick one that elicits strong negative feelings, maybe, fear or shame. Imagine it with as many sensory details as possible.

Example: Jack remembered the time when he got so anxious during a presentation that he froze. No words came out of his mouth while everyone gaped at him. Eventually, he had to excuse himself because he couldn't breathe anymore. This presentation was very important to him, and he had been preparing for it for months. He felt ashamed and disappointed in himself. He thought back to how eerie the silence felt as everyone expected him to say something, he remembers his heartbeat being so loud, he wondered if everyone in the room could hear it. After he walked out of the room, his feet barely supporting him, he dissolved into tears in the washroom.

2. **Write a new script.** Change the narrative of the memory leading to a positive outcome.

Example: Jack imagined when he froze, his manager stepped in and took over. The manager told everyone to take a 5-minute break and then reconvene. Once everyone left the room, he checked-in with Jack. He helped Jack calm down, told him he was doing great, and handed him a glass of water.

Jack took a few deep breaths and felt a bit better. By the time everyone came back, he was calm enough to continue the presentation.

3. **Mentally replay the new outcome.** Rehearse the new script over and over in your mind. Focus on your feelings of relief and being empowered.

4. **Reflect on the new experience.** How does this new script affect your thoughts and feelings?

For Jack, the new script made him feel like someone had his back, he felt supported. It made him feel that going forward, he should try to talk to his superior about his anxiety and seek help. He felt relieved with the alternate script and sensed the intensity of his feelings of shame had reduced a little. Imagery rescripting reduces the emotional impact of distressing memories by rewiring your brain. It allows you to practice new responses to old triggers, thereby reinforcing a more positive view.

ACTIVITY:
Imagery Based Rescripting

Do this for one of your distressing memories.

1. Identify a distressing (not traumatic) memory.

_____

_____

_____

2. Write a new script.

_____

_____

_____

3. Mentally replay the new outcome.

_____

_____

_____

4. Reflect on the new experience.

_____

_____

_____

Mindset Shifts

The second technique I taught Lilah was how to change her mindset, especially when it was primarily negative in nature. A deficit mindset focuses on what you lack, for example, 'I am not a good public speaker,' 'I cannot deal with this stress,' or 'I can never get past my breakup.' Although primarily focused on when working with students in the education sector, the importance of working on deficit mindset is gradually being recognized in leadership as well.[17] Shifting your mindset is applicable in all areas of life.

The growth mindset focuses on the fact that you can develop your abilities through learning, training, and hard work. For the above examples, this would look like, 'I am working on becoming a good public speaker', 'I can learn how to deal with the stress', or 'I am slowly but gradually moving towards healing after the breakup.' If you notice, the deficit mindset statements keep you locked into the idea of you having no control of the situation and the situations appearing fixed. The growth mindset statements, on the other hand, remind you of the control you can exercise in the situation and that there's hope at the end of the tunnel. Merely by changing how you think about the situation, you create a more positive inner dialogue. Think about some of your deficit mindset thoughts that often come up and try to change them to growth mindsets.

Example:
Deficit Mindset – I can't do anything right.
Growth Mindset – I am doing the best I can and I am constantly improving my skills.

ACTIVITY:
Mindset Shifts

Write down your deficit and growth mindsets below.

Deficit Mindset - _____

Growth Mindset - _____

Deficit Mindset - _____

Growth Mindset - _____

Future Self Visualization

The third CBT technique I taught Lilah was future self-visualization. This technique encourages you to visualize a positive future self to find motivation to change and to promote optimism. Steps for future self visualization:

1. **Visualize.** Imagine yourself in the future, having accomplished the things you wanted to.
   Example:
   "I see myself being in social situations without feeling anxious."

2. **Describe what you see.** Write down how you are behaving, handling difficult situations, what you are thinking, and how you are feeling.
   Example:
   "I see myself being invited to parties, getting along with people, initiat-

ing conversations. I can see the joy on my face, I am excited. I am proud of myself for having reached this point."

3. **Make an action plan.** Based on what you visualized, list actionable steps you can take now to become your future self.
Example:

- I will download a friendship app on my phone.
- I will text with one person on that app.
- I will talk on the phone with one person from the app.
- I will meet one person I feel comfortable with.

4. **Assess your plan periodically.** Are you progressing towards your future self? What needs to be done further?

ACTIVITY:
Future Self Visualization

Now try this for yourself.

1. Visualize.

2. Describe what you see:

_____

_____

_____

_____

3. Make an action plan:

- _____

- _____

-

-

-

4. Assess regularly.

This exercise helps you find the right direction and fosters hope, especially when you are doubting yourself or not finding enough motivation. Today, you have focused on shifting your mindset, affirming positive thoughts, and visualizing and working towards your future self. This part of the book has helped you work on your thoughts, feelings, and behaviors to alleviate negative emotions and foster positive behaviors.

Review and Reflect

Well done on making it for 3 consecutive weeks! You are doing great. As we approach the last week of this workbook, it is important to reflect and review all that you have worked upon to further strengthen your learnings. This is a time to pause, look at how far you have come and to applaud yourself for making the effort. Reflecting will help you understand what has been working for you and what hasn't, and tweak anything that needs to be changed. Let's get started.

ACTIVITY:
Review your Goals

Revisit Day 15 and track your progress on goals since then.

Goal 1

Goal: _____

Steps Taken:

Milestones achieved: _____

_____

Obstacles Faced: _____

Solutions: _____

Goal Adjustment: _____

Goal 2

Goal: _____

Steps Taken: _____

Milestones achieved: _____

Obstacles Faced: _____

Solutions: _____

Goal Adjustment: _____

Having done that, make sure to acknowledge and appreciate how far you have come, notice the progress you have made and the challenges you have overcome to reach here. Take a moment to celebrate your success so far, however small it may seem.

ACTIVITY:
Managing Anxiety & Fear

During the last few days, you have developed an understanding of anxiety and fear and how they show up in your life. You subsequently learnt to manage these emotions effectively. Let's reflect on your learning.

1. Did you understand your triggers (for anxiety and fear) better? List them down.

- _____

- _____

- _____

- _____

- _____

2. Think about all the techniques you have learnt to manage your anxiety and fear. What worked the best for you and why do you think that is?

    Example: Grounding worked the best for me because it gave me the pause I needed, slowed down my bodily reactions, and made me feel calm enough to then be able to work on my thoughts.

    _____

    _____

    _____

3. Were you able to use some of these techniques in your daily life? How did this impact your life?

    Example: I have been using mindful drinking daily during my evening coffee break. It really helps me relax and reset. I feel calm to take on the rest of my day.

    _____

    _____

    _____

4. Go back to day 18 and reflect how you used graded exposure to work on some of your fears. How far are you on your hierarchy? What are the small graded steps you have been able to take so far?

    Example: Rode an elevator for 3 floors with more than one person.

    _____

    _____

    _____

5. Have you noticed any change in the intensity of your fear?

    Example: Riding an elevator for 3 floors with more than one person was 7 on my scale. Currently it is 4.

    _____

    _____

    _____

6. As the next action step, choose one anxiety prevention technique that has worked for you and make sure to schedule it in your daily routine.

    Example: Continuing to practice mindful drinking every day.

    _____

    _____

    _____

Lastly, you identified and challenged your core beliefs, and did exercises for positive thinking.

ACTIVITY:
Restructuring Core Beliefs

Look back at your activity from Day 19 and assess where you are on the action plans you decided upon. Write down at least one core belief you challenged and replaced.

Core Schemas identified:

Example: I am worthless.

1. _____

2. _____

3. _____

Reframed schemas:

Example: Sometimes some people may criticize me, but there are others who see my worth and appreciate me for who I am.

1. _____

2. _____

3. _____

Progress on Action Plans:

Example: I asked my close friend in what way am I bringing value to her life. He told me that I am a very patient listener and he always comes to me when he needs to think things through. He feels I am a major support in his life.

1. _____

2. _____

3. _____

Restructured Core Belief:

Example: My friend (and possibly others) believe I am worthy and I hold an important place in his (their) life.

1. _____

2. _____

3. _____

ACTIVITY:
Positive Mindset

Write down the growth mindset that had the biggest impact on you? What are you working towards?

Example: "Every day I am inching closer to become the person I want to be." This growth mindset helps me look past my mistakes and focus on my learning and growth.

_____

_____

_____

_____

As you wrap up this reflection, remember the skills you are learning in this workbook are work in progress. These skills form your toolbox and are meant to assist you in your day-to-day life. The more you practice them, the quicker they will become habits. You are now well-equipped in understanding your emotions of anxiety and fear better, and have the skills to manage them. You're continuing to develop a positive mindset. In ending this reflection, say this out loud here, "I have the necessary skills to manage my negative emotions. With each passing day, I am learning and growing to become the best version of myself."

PART 6

Managing Your Anger and Depression

Now that you have worked on restructuring your deep-rooted schemas, and learned to have a more positive mindset, it's time to tackle two very common emotions-anger and sadness. Both these emotions can deeply impact your life in different domains – personal, professional, and social. When left unchecked, they can sabotage your goals. In this section, I will help you understand what triggers your anger, how depressive symptoms show up, and how you can effectively manage these emotions.

The next few days will help you reflect on your emotional triggers and give you tools to deal with them in an adaptive manner. Anger often has as its triggers- frustration, feelings of injustice, or expectations being unmet. Day 22, with its focus on anger, examines how and when anger shows up for you, and how it affects your behaviors and impacts your overall life. With an in-depth understanding of your anger and how it operates, you will be better equipped at managing it.

On day 23, you will make a specialized intervention plan to manage your anger by learning ways to communicate assertively, listen actively, relax your physical responses, and solve problems constructively. Depression, in contrast to anger, is fueled by negative, critical thoughts about self, others, or the future. On Day 24, you will identify your thoughts that trigger and continue to maintain depressive symptoms, challenge, and reframe them. Thereafter, you will learn behavioral techniques to reduce your feelings of sadness. Finally, you will practice self-compassion to reduce your negative self-talk and be more kind to yourself. By the end of this part, you would have developed practical skills to manage your anger and depression, allowing you to regulate your emotions better.

DAY 22:

Understanding Anger

Today we will explore and understand the nature of anger, and identify common triggers. We will also attempt to understand how anger impacts your thoughts, feelings, and behaviors. Once you understand your anger better, you will be able to learn to manage it well.

Anger is often looked upon as a negative emotion. However, it is a very natural emotional response to certain situations when you are feeling frustrated, threatened, or wronged. Anger operates as a mechanism to protect you and prevents you from being harmed. Imagine if you did not experience anger, people would take advantage of you by cutting you off in a queue or by taking your belongings. Anger, like anxiety, is an adaptive emotion. It only becomes a problem when it is left unchecked, leading to anger outbursts, conflicts in work or relationships, and harmful behaviors like getting into fights. There are two things to understand from how anger is interpreted from a cognitive behavioral therapy lens.

1. **Anger versus Aggression**

    Anger is a feeling which all of us experience. It is a useful emotion when limited to a certain intensity. Aggression is a behavior, which acts on the feeling of anger. Aggression might be verbal or physical, active, or passive. Regardless of how it is expressed, aggression is not healthy. As long as you are able to remember, 'I am angry, but I do not want to be aggressive', you are doing good.

2. Thoughts lead to feelings

Anger, like all other feelings, arises from our thoughts. Remember the thought-feeling-behavior model of CBT? Like other negative feelings, anger sometimes arises from negative automatic thoughts, cognitive distortions, or negative schemas. When emanating from a faulty line of thinking, anger can result from the misinterpretation of an event. By challenging these thoughts, you can reduce your anger.

Now that you are keeping the above two points in mind, let us try to identify the common triggers of your anger. Some common triggers are-

- When expectations are not met (self or others')

- Frustration with self or others

- Perceived injustice or wrong

- Feeling ignored or disrespected

- Not feeling in control of the situation

Like anxiety, anger also follows a cycle.

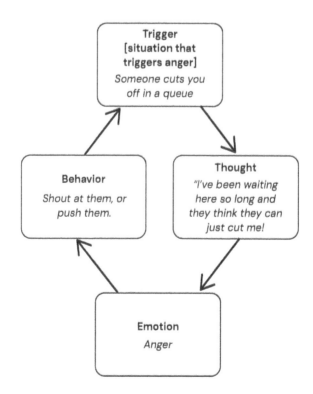

In the above example, the automatic thought, 'He thinks he's the only one whose time is important?' amplifies the anger leading to the consequent emotional and behavioral response. In the same example, if the person thought, 'Oh, he just cut me off. Why would he do that? Does he have a child waiting outside in a car?" the person's emotion might have been that of sympathy/ empathy and the consequent behavior being not saying anything.

In CBT, the goal is once again to challenge the automatic thoughts in order to change your feelings and behaviors that emanate from it. Some of the common cognitive distortions that result in anger include magnification ('she did it just to make me mad'), overgeneralization ('no one respects me, it is so frustrating'), or catastrophizing ('This person ruined my entire day by cutting me off in the queue'). In the above example, the person is engaging in the cognitive distortion of mindreading. If you are able to identify these distortions in your thinking and reframe them, you will not respond in a heightened emotional state.

However, sometimes anger flares up even before you have a moment to pause or think about not saying the first thing that came to your mind. At times like these, it would require a lot of self-control to stop, reflect, and reframe your thoughts. During these situations, the first step is to distance yourself from the situation, if possible, and then work on reducing the feeling of anger and the accompanying body sensations. I will discuss these techniques tomorrow when you learn how to manage your anger. It is extremely important to work on curtailing your anger outbursts to have an impact on your-

- **Physical health** – Anger triggers your blood pressure and heart rate, making it fatal at times. It could result in hypertension and heart disease.

- **Mental health** – Anger responses can lead to increased stress, frustration, and even feelings of guilt or regret after an outburst.

- **Relationships** – Anger outbursts can destroy relationships.

- **Professional Sphere** – Angry behaviors can cause conflicts at work and can affect your work performance or promotion opportunities.

- **Legal implications** – Extreme anger can also result in legal implications if you break something or harm someone.

ACTIVITY:
Understanding Your Anger

1. Think about a recent situation where you got angry. Write down your triggers, your thoughts, and your behaviors in that situation.

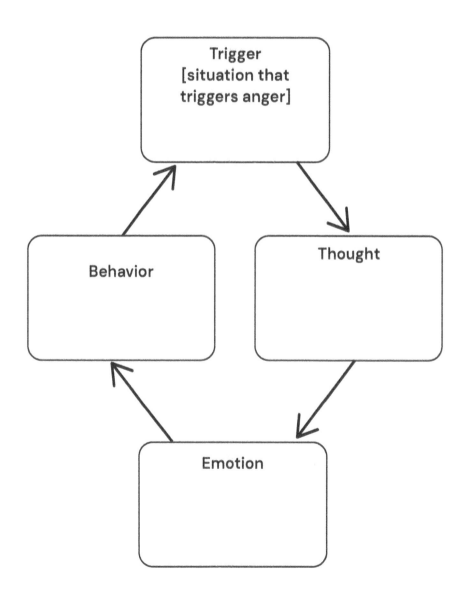

2. Can you identify any cognitive distortions in your thought?

*   _____

*   _____

*   _____

3. How has your anger impacted your life, in this situation or in any past
    situations? Any effects on your-

Mood -   _____

Work -   _____

Relationships - _____

Health -   _____

Today, you have understood what triggers your anger. You have identified cognitive distortions that often lead to the emotion of anger and explored
how anger impacts your life. Tomorrow, you will learn strategies to work on
your anger.

Managing Your Anger

We have established yesterday that anger is a normal human emotion but how you react in that situation makes it either constructive or destructive. With your understanding of how anger shows up for you, today we will be making a personalized plan for you to manage your anger. Let's begin with learning some strategies to manage your anger first. Once again, I will focus on addressing the relationship between thoughts, feelings, and behaviors, a core concept in CBT.

Yesterday, you identified some common cognitive distortions that might be playing a role in causing you to become angry. Let's start by challenging them as you have previously learned in this workbook. Use some of the ways from CRAFTED to challenge your thoughts. Ask yourself if you have any evidence for your thought or could there be an alternative explanation. Write down a more balanced thought instead. In the example from yesterday, it would look like "Maybe he didn't realize he cut me off. It's not personal." Does this new thought change your feelings in any way? Has the intensity of your anger lessened?

ACTIVITY:

Balanced Thinking

For the situation you identified yesterday, write down a more balanced thought.

_____

_____

How does this new thought make you feel? How angry do you feel about the situation now?

_____

_____

Assertive Communication

Assertive communication directly addresses thoughts that lead to anger, for example, "No one listens to me when I am calm, so I have to get angry for them to pay attention to me." Remember, some of the common triggers of anger, I discussed yesterday? These are-

- When expectations are not met (self or others')

- Frustration with self or others

- Perceived injustice or wrong

- Feeling ignored or disrespected

- Not feeling in control of the situation

With some of these, there could be a primary need which is not being fulfilled– the need to be respected and heard. While in the other scenarios, the situation itself seems frustrating leading to the feeling of loss and control and subsequent anger. In some of these instances, being assertive about your needs, standing up for yourself, and claiming control might be helpful to prevent the subsequent anger.

Assertive communication allows you to express your feelings and needs in a clear and respectful manner. Assertion serves as the bridge between being passive and being aggressive. If you are passive, everyone will walk over you. But being aggressive will not help the situation either. Both these are extreme responses. Being assertive gets the message across without any conflicts. Assertiveness means that you stand up for yourself and assert your rights without impinging on the rights of others. Let's learn some techniques for assertive communication.

Use "I" statements.

Imagine if someone says to you, "You have no respect for me. You never let me complete my sentences and are always smothering my voice." How would that make you feel? Most people immediately go into defensive mode and attack back, "Me? Why don't you look at your behavior?" And that's how an argument begins. The sentence came across as blaming so the other person immediately turns defensive and attacks back. Assertive communication is about expressing your needs and feelings instead of accusing the other. Using the above scenario, imagine if someone says to you, "I feel frustrated and hurt when I am not heard during our conversations. It makes me feel disrespected as if what I am saying is not important." How would this statement make you feel and how would you respond? Most people will focus on the other person being hurt and experience a sense of empathy. With no seemingly direct attack or blame to defend oneself from, you can actually look at the situation and be open to discuss it. This is a simple technique but proves to be very effective. The key is to shift from "you" statements to "I" statements and express feelings.

Be clear about your needs and expectations.

The cognitive distortion of mindreading comes up in a lot of conflictual scenarios where there is an expectation that the other person 'should know' in a sense of being able to read your mind. But it is an unreasonable expectation which lets you down and makes you feel frustrated. It is important to express your needs and expectations if you want them to be met. Be specific in your communication.

Example: "I need you to hear me out first and then I want to hear your perspective."

Monitor your tone and body language.

When a conversation is getting heated, it's not just our words that are impacted. Our tone, pitch, volume, body language, everything undergoes a transformation. This affects the other person and their communication as well. It is important to be mindful of these non-verbal gestures and make sure that your tone is calm and your body language is neutral. Feel free to express your thoughts in a manner that doesn't come across as aggressive or threatening to the other person.

Be prepared to listen.

During a conflict, listening is as important as stating your feelings. Listen actively to what is being said, be open-minded, try to understand their perspective. You can still choose to disagree but if you're able to make the other person feel heard, they will be more open to looking at your point of view. Try to use techniques like reflection and validation in the act of active listening.

- Reflection – like a mirror, you reflect back someone's words.

- Validation of feelings – Validate their emotions, even if you choose to disagree with their argument.

Example: "We really need to sell this bed before we move out and Sunday is the only day someone can come pick it up. We can sleep on the carpet. It's just one night. I am willing to adjust, why can't you? I am so frustrated."

"I am hearing that we need to sell the bed before we move out and no one is willing to come on Monday, they want to pick it up on Sunday. You're suggesting we sleep on the carpet and adjust for one night (Reflection). You're unable to understand why I can't sleep on the carpet for one night and that makes you feel frustrated (Validation of feelings). Even though it is just one night, I have had issues with my back previously and I do not want to jeopardize my physical health. I am willing to either give up the amount we will receive for the bed, or we can book a hotel for a night, whichever costs less, but sleeping on the carpet is not an option for me (Continuing to disagree).

This is a disagreement, with both people having differing opinions but using active listening skills, it is comparatively easier to avoid getting angry and to reach a resolution or a middle ground.

ACTIVITY:
Assertive Communication

Recall a recent argument or conflict you had with a friend, coworker, spouse etc. Focus on a situation where you felt your needs were not being met. Write down your typical response in that situation. Then, attempt to use assertive communication applying all of the techniques above. Write in as much detail, what you would change and how that communication will look like.

Example:

Situation: Argument with a friend because she never initiates contact. I am the one always texting, and messaging her.

Typical Response: Being passive-aggressive, reducing my texts and calls until I miss her. Then continue with calls but start to get angry or resentful on small things because of the piled-up anger.

New Response:

1. Asserting my needs and expectations

2. Using "I statements"

3. Active listening

4. Monitoring my tone and body language

I will call my friend and tell her in a calm tone, "I really enjoy talking to you, but I feel like I am the only one always initiating contact. It makes me feel sad and hurt. I feel like maybe I am not valued as much as I value you in my life." And then I will be open to her perspective and will listen actively. Now you try it here.

Situation:

_____

_____

_____

Typical Response:

_____

_____

_____

New Response:

_____

_____

_____

Relaxation Techniques

Anger results from our thoughts and shows up in our behaviors. But there is another component of anger- the physiological element. Increased heart rate, tensed muscles, and shallow breathing are some of the ways anger shows up in your body. The behavioral component of CBT focuses on teaching you relaxation techniques to reduce this element, thereby, having an impact on the anger response. On Day 17, you learned box breathing and mindfulness. Those strategies can be implemented to calm yourself down when feeling angry.

The first step is to be able to identify as soon as possible that you are feeling angry. The second step is to try to get some distance from the situation or person, if possible. Moving out of the room is helpful to prevent yourself from expressing anger in a harmful manner. Mindfulness helps you stay focused in the moment without judgment. You can observe your feelings without immediately reacting to the situation. Pay attention to how anger feels in your body and mind. Once you're able to do that, engage in box breathing or other relaxation techniques to calm yourself down.

You can also use Visualization technique if you are able to find a calm, quiet corner. Settle in and close your eyes. Imagine a place which makes you feel calm. This could be a forest, the ocean, top of a mountain, or even your own reading nook that you cannot access at the moment. Imagine you are there. Look around the sights. Focus on the sounds in that place. Are there any vivid smells you can notice? Visualization helps you get away from the situation in your mind and gives you the time and space to gain emotional control and prevents you from reacting.

Problem Solving

The last technique to manage your anger involves finding alternate ways of solving the problem that has come up. The aim of CBT is to help you shift from unproductive, anger-led reactions to constructive problem-solving. Anger stems from frustrations, a lot of which are outside your control. Using problem solving techniques helps you regain that control and take action steps to resolve it. Here are the steps to problem-solving-

1. **Identify and state the problem clearly.** What is making you angry?
    Example: "I get angry when I am interrupted while I am focusing on a task at work."

2. **Brainstorm solutions.** Think of all possible solutions.
    Example: "I could put up a notice informing colleagues not to disturb me, I could do my major focus tasks at a time when I am least likely to be disturbed, I could share this with my colleagues and find the best way to avoid this."

3. **Evaluate all the options you have come up with.** What are the pros and cons of each? Would it be realistic? Would it help?
    Example: "Putting up a notice might give out the message that I am arrogant. It's not realistically possible to focus only at a certain time. Talking to my colleagues might be helpful".

4. **Take action.** Based on your evaluation, decide the best possible action step, carry it out, and monitor results to check if your problem is solved. If it isn't', pick another solution from the above step and try that out instead.
    Example: "I will tell my colleagues that my focus gets interrupted and I need their help. Decide on a mutually agreeable way to let them know when not to disturb me (put 'busy' on my calendar, or decide on the best time they can approach me, making it a targeted time window unless it's something very important that can't wait)."

ACTIVITY:
Problem Solving

Now, follow the steps for a situation that needs to be solved.

1. What makes me angry?

_____

_____

_____

_____

2. Possible solutions

•
_____

•
_____

•
_____

3. Evaluate options

_____

_____

_____

_____

4. Final solution and take action

_____

_____

_____

_____

ACTIVITY:
Personalized Anger Management Plan

You have learned several techniques to manage your anger today. Let us make a personalized anger management plan for you.

Identified Cognitive Distortions that lead to anger

_____

_____

General Balanced Thought

_____

_____

During anger-provoking situations, I will

1. Step away

2. Calm myself down using techniques (Write down techniques that would work for you: relaxation/ visualization/ mindfulness)

_____

_____

3. Techniques I will use to communicate assertively (Which are the ones you are not typically using but want to continue learning to use?)

_____

_____

4. Use problem-solving techniques to resolve the issue.

- _____

- _____

- _____

- _____

- _____

You have now learnt to manage your anger using cognitive and behavioral strategies. In the next chapter, we will work on managing feelings of sadness.

Coping with Depression

Depression appears as a heavy weight that makes seemingly simple tasks impossible to execute. It gets harder to get out of bed in the morning, take a shower, or do the dishes. You feel hopeless, demotivated, and stuck. It is difficult to explain to people why you can't seem to get out of the house, are putting on weight, and can't focus on anything. Every little thing feels like a mountain to be moved. Depression or depressive symptoms are characterized by[18]:

- Feelings of sadness,

- Change in appetite – eating less or more, weight loss or gain,

- Change in sleep patterns – sleeping less or more, disturbed sleep, waking up early, problems falling asleep,

- Decreased social interaction,

- Low energy,

- Unable to experience interest or pleasure in most activities,

- Feelings of worthlessness or guilt,

- Reduced ability to focus.

On a severe level, thoughts of death or suicide are also prominent. If you are experiencing serious depressive symptoms, please contact your nearest emergency care center. This workbook is only meant to be considered for people with depressive symptoms of a milder level. You can also use these exercises to manage generalized feelings of sadness that we all experience on a regular basis.

Depression is maintained by the thought-feeling-behavior cycle. Using CBT, the idea is to break this cycle by working on the thoughts, physical symptoms, and behaviors in order to improve mood and restore motivation and function. Throughout this workbook, you have learnt several techniques proven to be useful for depressive symptoms. I will show you how to apply them here while also teaching you new strategies to specifically deal with depressive symptoms. Today, you will learn how to deal with sadness and other symptoms of depression to help regain control of your mood. Let's use techniques you learned previously in this workbook to see how they would specifically apply to symptoms of depression. Take the example of Carl.

Carl was feeling sad and had not talked to or met anyone for the last week as he felt he had no energy to have a conversation. While trying to understand some of the thoughts Carl experienced which might be maintaining his feelings of sadness, he mentioned, "I was unable to get the last project my team and I had worked so hard for. My colleagues counted on me. Not only did I fail terribly, I also let them down. I don't know how to face them anymore." Using CBT, Carl identified his cognitive distortions (catastrophizing, magnification), and challenged his thoughts. We then tried to identify his cognitive schemas (Day 19). Carl realized he had always felt like a failure, never good enough, as no matter what he did, he could not come up to the expectations of his father. He was not the best in his class, didn't get the highest grades, and had no aptitude or interest in being an entrepreneur, something that his father wanted for him. No matter what he did, he was never praised or encouraged. Over time, he internalized being not good enough and being a failure.

In our sessions together, Carl was able to talk about this internalization and shared more incidents that solidified this for him. We then used the CRAFTED technique to challenge some of his thoughts and to positively reframe them. He reminded himself of all his achievements and the progress he had made in his life so far, which was contrary to his thinking that he was a failure. He acknowledged that his father has different expectations of him which he was not able to fulfill completely. But he looked at evidence from other people, including his mother, sister, colleagues and friends who would congratulate him on his achievements, praise and admire him. He was able to reframe his thought as, "We were unable to get this project and it is disappointing and saddening. But all of us, including me, tried our best. In the past, we have got other projects and we can continue to apply for more in the future. My colleagues have seen me working hard and they are disappointed at the outcome and not disappointed in me."

Having reframed his thought, he was able to decide on the action step to go to his workplace the next morning even though he didn't feel like it. He reminded himself that no one was disappointed in him, he was not a failure, and he needed to start working on his next goal now to achieve it.

ACTIVITY:
Reframing your Thoughts

Try doing this with one of your thoughts now.

Situation (what made me feel sad/ depressed?):

_____

_____

Thought:

_____

_____

Cognitive Distortion:

_____

_____

Cognitive Schema:

_____

_____

Challenge the thought:

_____

_____

Reframe the thought:

_____

_____

Action Step:

_____

_____

Activity Scheduling

Depression leads to reduction in activities that were previously pleasurable. The lack of these activities further maintains the feelings of sadness. Using the activity scheduling component of CBT, you will be planning and scheduling activities that you found enjoyable and meaningful to help you break the cycle of inactivity.

Activity scheduling is a part of what you learnt on Day 12 based on the idea that even though you may not feel like it, when you do engage in previously pleasurable activities, it will improve your mood and energy. When facing depressive symptoms, there is a lack of energy, and you feel I will act when I have more energy. This keeps you on the never-ending loop. In order to get out of the loop, you need to take action steps to improve your mood. Here are the steps for activity scheduling-

1. Identify enjoyable activities (you can use the list you made on Day 12 or add to it).

2. Create a realistic plan. Be mindful of how much time and energy you have. Do not go overboard in planning.

Example:
"I will go for a walk for 15 minutes after dinner."

3. Rate your mood before and after the activity to monitor any change.

4. Gradually increase the number, frequency and duration of pleasurable activities.

ACTIVITY:
Create your Activity Schedule

Identify one pleasurable activity to engage in for each day of the week. Rate your mood before and after each activity.

Day	Activity	Mood Before (1-10)	Mood After (1-10)
Monday			
Tuesday			
Wednesday			
Thursday			
Friday			
Saturday			
Sunday			

Self-Compassion

One of the consequences of depressive symptoms is self-criticism, low self-esteem, and lack of confidence. CBT encourages you to have more compassionate self-talk to reduce negative emotions.

Here are steps to building self-compassion.

1. **Monitor your self-talk.** How do you talk to yourself? Do you use any labels when thinking about yourself? ("I am stupid, I am such a fool")

2. **Be aware of negative self-talk.** When you find yourself thinking critically about yourself, take a pause.

3. **What would you say to a friend in this situation?** Would you react differently if a friend was facing these circumstances? (I will tell him, "It's not your fault. These things happen. You will do better next time. Don't let this bring you down.")

4. **Jot down self-compassionate statements.** "I am trying my best. It's alright to make mistakes, I am only human."

5. **Practice speaking more kindly to yourself.** Do not judge yourself.

ACTIVITY:
Building Self-Compassion

1. Are there any negative labels you use for yourself? Or any negative self-talk?

_____

_____

_____

_____

2.   What would you say to a friend in this situation?

_____

_____

_____

_____

3.   Write down self-compassionate statements.

_____

_____

_____

_____

Social Support

As mentioned above, during depression, you may not feel like talking to anyone and might have less energy. But cutting out social interaction leads to isolation and decreased level of social support, which again, continues to maintain depressive symptoms. Having social support and reaching out to your loved ones ensures a positive impact on your mood and well-being.

ACTIVITY:
Seeking Social Support

Here are the steps to enlist the help of your support system.

1.   Write down a list of people you can talk to (family, friends, a coach, a therapist).

- _____

- _____

- _____

- _____

2. Make small social goals.

Example: I will text this friend or call that family member or schedule a session with my coach.

1. _____

2. _____

3. _____

4. _____

5. _____

3. Take action steps by either scheduling it in your calendar or setting reminders on your phone. It might seem difficult and daunting. Begin with smaller steps but make it happen.

   Apart from the techniques you have learnt today, there are other techniques that help with depressive symptoms which you have already learnt in this workbook. Refer back to them and utilize as many as possible-

- Mindfulness Exercises (Day 17)

- Problem Solving (Day 23)

- Relaxation (Day 17)

PART 7

Nurturing Self-Acceptance and Building your Future

You are now better equipped to manage several negative emotions, like anxiety, fear, anger, and sadness. Throughout this workbook, you have learnt a lot and are growing into the best version of yourself. But amidst all these changes for the better, you also need to be able to find self-acceptance for who you are. Self-acceptance is tied to your emotional well-being, as it places the emphasis on internal rather than external validation. When your focus is on external accomplishments, a single setback can make you feel unworthy or incapable. Thus, in this final section, the focus is to acknowledge your strengths and build a positive self-image. Several of the feelings I have discussed in this workbook have impacted your self-esteem. Now it's time to appreciate and accept yourself for who you are.

On Day 25, I will guide you to focus on your strengths and to avoid comparing yourself to others. This day asks you to focus on your achievements and successes and let go of some of the unnecessary pressure you put on yourself. It is important to accept yourself, as who you are, in this moment, without judgment. Day 26 will help you deepen your self-acceptance with the help of mindful breathing and taking a self-compassion break. Self-compassion reminds you to be as kind to yourself as you would be to a friend.

CBT is not merely applicable to the areas mentioned so far in the workbook. The techniques of CBT are also applicable to problems that might not have specifically been discussed, like managing stress, or other negative emotions, and effectively managing personal conflicts. These will be discussed on Day 27 to equip with long-lasting emotional resilience. By using these techniques in other areas of your life, you will pave the way for personal growth.

On the last day of this workbook, you will focus on how to integrate your learning and develop a plan to continue to utilize your learnings on a daily basis. This final day helps you bring together everything you have learnt so far, ensuring that your progress continues beyond the workbook. Remember, this workbook is just the beginning- your journey towards self-acceptance, growth and development continues over a lifetime.

On the last day of this workbook, you will focus on how to integrate your learning and develop a plan to continue to utilize your learnings on a daily basis. This final day helps you bring together everything you have learnt so far, ensuring that your progress continues beyond the workbook. Remember, this workbook is just the beginning- your journey towards self-acceptance, growth and development continues over a lifetime.

Building Self-Esteem

Today, the focus is on building self-esteem by challenging self-criticism and developing a more balanced, positive view of yourself. We are often our harshest critics. Your negative thoughts about yourself undermine your confidence and self-worth. When these thoughts are not countered against, they become automatic and influence your life on a daily basis.

Low self-esteem leads to negative thinking patterns and negative self-talk, contributing directly to symptoms of anxiety and depression. Using CBT, you will identify and address negative thoughts that lead to self-criticism and reframe them into positive thoughts.

Self-esteem is the way in which you look at and think about yourself. Thoughts like 'I am not good enough,' 'I am stupid,' 'I can never do anything right' contribute to a low self-esteem. These beliefs, like many others, are formed from childhood based on early life experiences. These are further reinforced by external feedback, perfectionistic tendencies, and self-criticism. Using CBT techniques, you will work on these thoughts. Pay close attention to how you think about yourself. The goal is not to criticize yourself but to recognize these negative thoughts about yourself before you change your internal dialogue to be more kind, supportive, and compassionate. One of the ways you will do this is by using your learning from earlier days and challenging and reframing these thoughts. Here are the steps-

1. **Identify critical thoughts.** It was important to Thomas that everything around him should be perfect. He loved being organized and meticulous. He spent hours on a single document, fine tuning it until he was satisfied. He faced several challenges at his workplace due to this behavior. He never handed work in on time, missed deadlines, and was reprimanded often. But to him, if everything wasn't perfect, it didn't matter. With continuous complaints and negative feedback, he began lacking confidence in his abilities. He felt like he couldn't do anything right. "I'm such a failure." was one of his critical thoughts.

2. **Identify the cognitive distortion.** Thomas was engaging in an all or none thinking error which kept up his perfectionistic tendencies. His subsequent thought of "I am a failure" represented the cognitive distortions of overgeneralization and magnification.

3. **Challenge the criticism.** Through our sessions together, Thomas challenged his criticisms- "Is it okay to discount everything that I have done just because it's not perfect according to me?" "Because I got delayed on my deadline, does it really mean I am a failure?" Thomas also used the CRAFTED technique to further challenge his thought. He was able to find (contrary) evidence of areas in which he was a success – "When a task requires an eye for detail, I am the one my manager approaches, and I have not disappointed him in this regard, even once."

4. **Reframe the statement.** Based on the challenging statements, Thomas was able to reframe his critical thoughts – "Things go wrong sometimes, not everything can be perfect all the time, despite my best efforts." "Sometimes things don't work out and it's okay."

5. **Develop self-affirming thoughts.** He developed affirming thoughts like "I am trying my best and that's enough.", "I am continually learning from my mistakes."

ACTIVITY:
Reframe Self-Critical Thoughts

Now attempt this with one of your self-critical thoughts.

1. Identify the critical thought.

_____

_____

_____

_____

2. Identify the cognitive distortion.

_____

_____

_____

_____

3. Challenge the criticism.

_____

_____

_____

_____

4. Reframe the statement.

_____

_____

_____

_____

5. Develop self-affirming thoughts.

_____

_____

_____

_____

Strengths Inventory

Often, as a self-critical individual, you tend to focus on your mistakes and weaknesses. From a CBT framework, the concept of strength-based thinking is helpful in building self-esteem. The idea is to shift the focus from weaknesses while encouraging you to look for and acknowledge your strengths. This strengths-based approach helps you recognize your positive attributes in order to counteract self-sabotaging thoughts and enhance your self-esteem.

When you focus on your strengths, you automatically challenge cognitive distortions like overgeneralization ("I can't do anything right.") or minimization ("Oh, there must not have been enough applicants, that's why I got this job."). The human brain has a natural tendency for negative bias. You are more likely to remember negative events than positive ones. If I asked you right now, can you recall some situations where you were embarrassed, I am sure you could quickly come up with several.

When you focus on your strengths, you are engaging in cognitive reframing, a core component of CBT that shifts your mindset from overly critical to a more balanced one. Through the following exercise, the idea is to help you identify and become aware of your strengths. Here are the steps to follow-

1. **Identify your strengths.** Think about your positive qualities, past achievements or skills you possess. Small wins and achievements are just as important as the big ones.

    Example: "I am a patient listener.", "I am good with finances." or "I am a reliable friend."

You can also think of basic daily actions when you helped a stranger or managed your responsibilities well and extrapolate your strengths from these incidents.

Example: "I helped a tourist with directions (I am helpful)." or "I finished all my tasks today (I am committed to my responsibilities)."

Try looking for strengths in different areas of your life-

- Personal Strengths. Are you passionate? Creative? Compassionate? Generous?

- Professional Strengths. Are you committed? Motivated? Do you have strong communication skills? What about your negotiation skills? Are you good at sales? Are you organized? Do people look up to you to solve work-related problems?

- Social Strengths. Are you a good listener? A supportive friend? Do you have great communication skills?

2. **Ask for feedback.** Sometimes we are unaware of some of our strengths. Ask your loved ones or colleagues about what they feel your strengths are, what they admire about you. This feedback is really helpful to shift how you think about yourself.

3. **Reflect on your strengths.** Think about how you developed these strengths over time and how they helped you overcome obstacles in life or supported you through tough times. Think about how you can build on these strengths or use them to overcome hurdles in the future.

Example: "Because I am such a good listener, people open up to me. They look forward to spending time with me. On the basis of this, I have been able to make great personal and professional relationships. These people have helped me in times of need. I can continue to be this person and work on developing deeper relationships." The goal is not just to acknowledge and appreciate your strengths but to view them as resources to fall back upon when needed. Strength-based thinking helps you improve your self-competence and self-esteem.

ACTIVITY:
Focus on Your Strengths

1. Write down some of your strengths.

    - _____
    - _____
    - _____
    - _____

2. Write down your strengths, based on feedback from others.

    - _____
    - _____
    - _____
    - _____

3. Reflect on your strengths.

    _____

    _____

    _____

    _____

Avoiding Comparison

Another important factor in building self-esteem is letting go of comparison with others. When you compare yourself to others, you usually pitch your weaknesses to their strengths. That is unfair to yourself and leads to feelings of inadequacy and resultant low self-esteem. For example, you might think, "He is more successful than me," or "All of my friends are married, and I don't even have a girlfriend." The idea is to focus on and track your journey rather than comparing it with others.

ACTIVITY:
Success Journaling

This technique encourages you to track your daily successes, no matter how small. It instills a habit of focusing on your strengths and achievements in your daily life. It also helps you reflect on your past and present self, instead of comparing yourself to others.

1. Pick a journal for your daily tracking.

2. Before bedtime, reflect back on your day and write down things you did well or achieved. Did you complete any task? Did you get praised for one of your abilities or any success in the workplace?

    Example: "I balanced my work and leisure time today." or "My manager complimented me on my great presentation today."

    Think back over your day yesterday. Write some of your successes below.

    _____

    _____

3. Reflect weekly. During the weekend, spend some time looking over your achievements of the week. Compare your journey from last week to this week. A healthy comparison is the one that you have between your past and present self.

This journal is also a tool for you to revisit when you are struggling with your self-esteem or being too hard on yourself. When you regularly identify and acknowledge your successes, you notice a shift in your self-talk which directly impacts your self-esteem.

'Should' Statements

Words like 'should' and 'must,' more often than not, carry a burden of unrealistic expectations, eventually leading to failure and a negative impact on self-esteem. Statements like, "I should be married by now" or "I must always be in control of the situation." create unnecessary pressure stemming from rigid rules created by the society or others that you are trying to adhere to. Sometimes, this pressure could also be of your own making. It is important to recognize and reframe these thoughts.

Example:
"I would prefer to have a partner by now but it's alright that it is taking me longer to find the right partner for myself." or "I would prefer to be in control, but I understand that sometimes the situation is outside of my control."

Letting go of these 'should' and 'must' statements help you adopt a more realistic and compassionate approach to yourself, paving the way for a healthier self-esteem.

ACTIVITY:
Reframing 'Should' Statements

1. Identify your 'Should' and 'Must statements. Write them below.

_____

_____

_____

_____

2. Reframe the above statements. Replace 'should' and 'must' with 'could' and 'prefer'.

_____

_____

_____

_____

Building self-esteem by breaking off negative self-talk and reframing how you think about yourself is a gradual and continuous process. Be patient and kind with yourself while you continue to work on this each day.

DAY 26:

Nurturing Self-Acceptance

Self-acceptance goes a step beyond self-esteem. It focuses on accepting yourself for who you are, all your strengths and weaknesses included. Self-acceptance means you love yourself regardless of success or failure in life. This is not complacency or indulgence. It is an unconditional positive regard for yourself.

Inculcating self-acceptance using CBT means not letting your negative thoughts define your self-worth. Self-acceptance asks you to recognize the difference between who you are and what you do. You are more than your actions. For example, making a mistake does not mean that you are a failure. It only means that as a human, you make mistakes, and that's okay. You can continue to learn and grow. CBT encourages you to reduce judgment-based thinking and have a more realistic and kind assessment of yourself.

Self-acceptance helps to regulate emotions of shame, guilt, and frustration. It is when you fail to accept yourself for who you are, that you engage in cognitive distortions like magnification, labeling, or all-or-none thinking. For example, when you label yourself a failure based on one mistake, you engage in a magnification error, thereby judging yourself. Today, I will build on some techniques you have already learnt in general, using the principles of mindfulness and self-compassion. Let us learn some specific techniques to work on this.

Self-Compassion Break

Often, when something goes wrong, self-criticism comes as an automatic thought, and it gets difficult to break out of that cycle. During those times, it is important to take a self-compassion break. This exercise is so powerful because of the concept of neuroplasticity, which I have talked about earlier in this workbook. When you engage in repetitive self-criticism, your brain pathways learn this connection, and generalize it to all situations, thereby hampering several of your life domains. You start doubting yourself as a son, a husband, an employee, and a colleague. The self-compassion break helps to break the cycle of negative thinking.

The steps are as follows-

1. **Acknowledge the present state.** Acknowledge the stress, pain, and difficult situation you are experiencing in the present.

   Example: "I am feeling overwhelmed." "It is too much to handle."

2. **Practice Kindness.** As if talking to a friend, be kind and compassionate and use supportive statements.

   Example: "It is okay to feel overwhelmed, it is a tough situation."

3. **Connect with humanity.** Remind yourself you are not the only one struggling. All of us find ourselves in tough moments. Feel connected to others. "I am not alone in experiencing this."

ACTIVITY:
Taking a Self-Compassion Break

Acknowledge your present state:

_____

_____

_____

_____

Practice kindness:

_____

_____

_____

_____

Connect with humanity:

_____

_____

_____

_____

ACTIVITY:
Self-Acceptance Affirmations

Self-acceptance affirmations are intentional statements that are meant to challenge your beliefs about yourself. In CBT, these affirmations are used to restructure unhelpful thinking patterns by encouraging compassion for the self. Example- "I accept myself for who I am." "I deserve to be loved for who I am." By regularly practicing these affirmations, you can alter the way you think about yourself, leading to a strong sense of self-worth.

Write down your affirmations.

1. _____

2. _____

3. _____

4.

5.

It is helpful to say out loud some of these affirmations on a regular basis, especially when you can access a mirror and look yourself in the eye while saying them.

Self-Compassion Letter

Imagine a time when you were critical or harsh with yourself. Write a letter to yourself based on what you would tell a friend who was caught in a similar situation. Offer words of support and encouragement.

Example:
"Dear Sofia,

I am aware how hard the last few days have been for you. It was extremely disappointing when your ideas were not heard during the work meeting. You felt like you were reprimanded, and your ideas were shot down. I know you have been feeling weak and useless ever since that incident. You feel that you have done everything possible in the last 3 years in this organization. Despite that, your hard work is not acknowledged. You feel dispensable and that hurts. I know a part of you feels like "what's the point? No matter what I do, it's never enough." But I want to remind you of your achievements. Remember years ago, when you wanted to get into medical school and worked so hard to get that degree. Getting a job in this organization was a dream come true. Remember how many candidates applied for this one position? You were the one who got in, based on your qualifications, and performance. You have achieved so much, and you are continuing to grow. I am so proud of how far you have come. I am so happy with the person you have become. It's okay if not everyone can see the worth of your ideas. It does not take away your worth or value. People are different and have differing views. It's okay to not always be on the same page. I want you to know, remember, and acknowledge your worth, regardless of anyone seeing it or not. You matter. You are worthy. You are valuable."

ACTIVITY:

Self-Compassion Letter

Write yourself a Self-compassion letter.

_____

_____

_____

_____

_____

_____

_____

_____

_____

_____

_____

_____

_____

_____

By engaging in self-compassion, you are building new healthy pathways in your brain towards a positive self-image and self-acceptance. Remember, self-acceptance does not mean you stop learning and growing. It means accepting and loving yourself for who you are while continuing to grow. Neuroplasticity tells you that change is possible at any age. By accepting yourself for who you are, you are not only working on your mental health but also changing the way your brain functions!

Applying CBT to Other Life Areas

As you near the end of this workbook, I want you to recognize and remember that the skills you have learned are not only applicable to specific issues like anxiety, fear, self-esteem, and depression that we have focused on. These tools have a far-reaching application to other domains of your life leading to generalized well-being and better quality of life.

Using the lessons from this workbook, you can also positively impact other areas of your life like regulating your emotions and reducing your stress levels. Several of the strategies you have learnt so far can be applied in other areas of your life including managing emotional and behavioral concerns. CBT techniques are versatile and flexible and can be used to positively impact various domains of your life. By using CBT techniques, you can impact your:

- **Stress.** When stressed, you can use the box breathing and grounding techniques to manage your emotions. You can also try to identify if there are any cognitive distortions that are making you feel more stressed about the situation than is optimal. Once you do that, you can challenge and positively reframe them, thereby, reducing your stress. You can also utilize the technique of activity scheduling to break down a task into smaller goals that seem comparatively easier to achieve.

- **Emotional Regulation.** With techniques like mindfulness, you learn to give yourself the space and time to be in the here and now. This will help you become more aware of your emotions in the moment, thereby, being better at regulating them, when the need arises.

- **Relationships and Communication.** Using assertive communication can have a significant positive impact on both your personal and professional life. In the face of conflicts or misunderstanding, using 'I' statements and engaging in active listening would immediately reduce the tension and lend itself to an amicable resolution. Cognitive schemas like 'No one loves me,' or 'Everybody abandons me,' often causes insecurity which impacts personal relationships. By working on restructuring these schemas using CBT, you are setting the ground for harmonious and healthy relationships.

- **Physical and Mental Health.** When you engage in pleasurable activities and ensure activity scheduling, you are developing positive lifestyle habits like eating nutritious food, exercising, or having skin care routines. These impact your health in a positive manner. Engaging in relaxation activities and mindfulness are effective in ensuring better sleep, reducing stress levels, and encouraging a here and now approach.

Look back at some of your concerns from earlier in the workbook. Is there some other domain you would like to work on?

ACTIVITY:
Managing a New Concern

1. Identify the area to work on.
2. Select the technique best suited to manage it.
3. Use the technique.
4. Write your observations and track progress.

Example:

1. Stress, especially when the deadlines are coming up.

2. Box Breathing and Grounding

3. When I am stressed, I will take out 5 minutes to either box breathe or ground myself.

4. The techniques helped me lower my heart rate, reduced sweating and helped me focus back on my task after I spent 5 minutes doing them.

1. Area of concern:

_____

2. Technique:

_____

_____

3. Action Step:

_____

_____

4. Track Progress:

_____

_____

By utilizing already learnt techniques, you can impact several areas of your life. Keep practicing them to find more confidence and control in your ability to manage negative thoughts and emotions.

Integrating CBT into Daily Life

On the last day of this workbook, it is important to develop a plan for how you are going to continue practicing the CBT techniques you learnt and continue to benefit from this workbook. CBT is not merely a therapeutic tool. Through this workbook, I aimed to bring CBT to your daily life so even though we have come to the end of the workbook, your progress should continue. The aim of this workbook was to bring long-lasting change in the areas of your life to ensure your personal growth. You have done so much in the last 4 weeks, but in order to have a lasting effect, you need to integrate CBT in your daily life. Let's create a daily routine, utilizing CBT principles.

ACTIVITY:
Daily Routine

1. **Mindfulness.** Start your day with a breathing or mindfulness technique. It could be as less as 5 minutes, but this will give you a calm start to the day and you will notice a positive impact on the rest of your day.

Example: Practice mindful breathing for 5 minutes first thing in the morning.

Add a reminder on your phone right now.

2. **Thought Tracking.** Carry a notebook or have a notes app on your phone to make a note of negative thoughts that come up for you during the day. You have learnt to reframe them but that can only be done once you are aware of these thoughts. The earlier you are able to notice them, the sooner you can reframe them. To begin with, you can put random reminders on your phone to alert you at various times of the day, to check-in with your thoughts.

Prepare your notebook or your notes app, and put these reminders.

3. **Nightly Reflection.** Before bed, reflect on the day and if you used any CBT techniques. Reflect on your progress, make goals, and identify any areas you want to work on the next day and decide action steps.

Prepare your journal, put a reminder.
Use of CBT today.
Example: I used mindful breathing when I was stressed before an important meeting.

Small goal for tomorrow, CBT technique to be used and action step.
Example: Express gratitude to a colleague in the office tomorrow.

ACTIVITY:
Monthly Check-in

Now that you know the whole process from goal setting to achieving them, make a list of your goals each month, track your progress and achieve them.

Example:
This month, I will focus on using assertive communication at my office.

SMART Goal(s) for this month and CBT Technique(s) I will use:

_____

_____

_____

Track your progress at month end, identify obstacles, propose solutions and set future action steps.

Example:
I practiced assertive communication with my colleagues. A few of them expressed surprise at my new behaviors but they appreciated it and said that they always thought I was a pushover and now they could see I was working on setting my boundaries.

_____

_____

_____

When you utilize CBT techniques on a daily basis and continue to check-in every month, you are setting a ground to continue to progress and develop. CBT is not a one-time fix. With constant use of these techniques, you are bringing positive changes in several domains of your life.

Conclusion

A huge congratulations on completing this CBT workbook! You made it! I am so proud of you, and you should be too. Over the past 4 weeks, you have been consistent and diligent in understanding yourself better and growing and transforming through this journey. Take a moment to pat yourself on the back.

When you began this workbook, you were struggling with depression, anxiety, fear, low self-esteem, or some other area of concern that was negatively impacting your life. Each day, you learned new skills to understand your thoughts, feelings, and behaviors and to manage them effectively.

Keep up your continued progress utilizing some of the daily and monthly check-ins you decided on. Keep a journal where you can jot down your goals, thoughts, and progress. Recognize that while self-help is a powerful tool, seeking help from a coach or therapist on a one-to-one basis would enhance your progress. Especially if you feel your concerns are of a more severe intensity, please do reach out to a professional. It is okay to ask for support while continuing to take steps to work on your growth.

As you move forward, continue to set new goals, and utilize the CBT techniques to help you progress on those goals. Remember growth is a life-long process and setbacks happen. Do not let them deter you. Continue to be kind, patient and compassionate with yourself on this journey. I sincerely thank you for trusting me and this process. I wish you continued success in your journey towards growth and development!

Before Continuing Your Journey

Thank you for taking the time to go through this book I sincerely hope the exercises have been beneficial to you.

I have a question, would you be willing to help someone else discover this too if all it cost was less than 60 seconds of your time?

If you would that's amazing! All you have to do is give an honest review on Amazon for this book. It's a simple act but for small publishers it provides an incredible amount of support.

It would be more than worth it if it could help even just one more person struggling with mental health, anxiety, or depression. To do that, and to keep it as quick and easy as possible, please scan a QR code with your cell phone's camera and press the link that comes up to go directly to your amazon review page.

Another option if you don't want to use the link is to head to your Amazon orders page, locate this book, and and click the "Write a Product Review" option. Thank you so much for your time. It really does go a long way towards helping more people discover CBT and these resources.

Review Amazon US

Review Amazon UK

Review Amazon Canada

Bonus Chapter: CBT Toolbox

This bonus chapter provides you with additional CBT tools to assist you in your journey towards mental well-being. Each tool in this toolbox is meant to complement the techniques you have already learnt in the workbook, ensuring you continue to build resilience, regulate your emotions, and work on self-awareness. This toolbox is your personal resource toolkit- full of strategies to continue to help you manage emotions like anxiety or teach you adaptive coping behaviors. These tools are not meant for a one-time use. Just as you go to the gym regularly to maintain your physical health, you need to return to these exercises over and over again until they become a part of your daily routine.

In the workbook, you tackled your negative thinking and emotions and established healthy ways of coping. You built an insight into your mental and emotional world by introspecting. In the toolbox, you will find a variety of tools for different purposes. Some might help you manage your anxiety, others may be focused on self-acceptance or developing useful behaviors. The idea is that through the use of the workbook, you would have been able to identify your goals and in what domains you need to continue to work on. You are now encouraged to recognize the tools that would be helpful for you and use them consistently. Check which tool resonates with you and incorporate it (them) into your daily routine.

The idea behind introducing these tools at this point is to help you remember the work of CBT (restructuring thoughts, managing anxiety and depression, building positive coping mechanisms) is an ongoing process. Your progress should not end at the end of this workbook. These are practices you can revisit over and over again. This toolbox is meant to aid your future journey and to support your ongoing development.

TOOL 1:

Behavior Chain Analysis

This CBT tool helps you recognize the steps that lead up to a dysfunctional behavior, like an emotional outburst, avoidance or addiction behaviors, or unhealthy coping mechanisms. Behavior Chain analysis also helps you understand what maintains or reinforces the consequences from this behavior. Here are the steps for Behavior Chain Analysis-

Step 1: Identify the problem behavior.
What is it that I want to change?
Example: emotional eating, procrastination, substance use (alcohol, nicotine etc.), or anger outbursts.

Step 2: Trace the chain back to get to the prompting event.
Which thoughts, feelings, or behaviors led me here?
Example: Right before my emotional eating episode, I had received a call from my mother letting me know that she will be visiting me this weekend.

Step 3: Examine the links in the chain of events.
What leads you to the problem behavior?
These could be your thoughts, physical sensations, feelings, actions, or events in the environment.
A (Actions)
B (Body Sensations)
C (Cognitions/ thoughts)
E (Events)

F (Feelings)

Example:

- I felt alarmed (Feeling) when my mother mentioned she would be coming over (Event).

- After I got off the phone, I thought, "I need to clean the house, otherwise she will criticize me on how messy everything is" (Cognition).

- The idea of having to clean up the house made me anxious (Feeling), my heart rate rose, I could notice my heart thudding loudly against my chest (Body sensation).

- I realized I also need to stock up my groceries or she would say "What do you eat, there is nothing in the kitchen." I also need to do something about my appearance (get a haircut, get a manicure, take a waxing appointment) because my mom is sure to find a way to criticize and ridicule me (Cognition).

- Everything seemed overwhelming and I just couldn't deal with it (Feeling).

- In order to ease the anxiety, I ordered a pizza and ate all of it in one sitting (Action).

Step 4: Identify vulnerability factors.

What things about myself or my situation made me more vulnerable?

Example: I was already having a stressful day at work when my mom called me.

Step 5: Notice the consequences.

What resulted from my behavior in myself and/ or my environment?

Example:

Short-term – I felt full and bloated. My stomach ached and I couldn't sleep for a long time.

Long term – I will gain weight and mom will find another reason to chastise me.

Step 6: Make a Prevention Plan.

(How can I reduce my vulnerability in the future? How can I prevent the prompting event from happening?)

Example: I can learn skills to manage my workplace stress and put them into action. I can either not pick up my mom's call in the middle of my stressful day or be able to set my boundaries and assert that it's not a good time to visit me this weekend, I have a lot on my plate.

Step 7: Adopt healthier strategies for each link in the chain.
Use the ABCEF list.

Example:

- Listen to why my mother wants to visit (Action).

- Let her know I am having a really stressful day at work and can I confirm with her in a few hours (Action).

- After I get off the phone, take deep, calming breaths (A) to reduce my anxiety (Body sensation, Feeling).

- Think about how I can assertively communicate with my mother (Cognition).

- Call her and let her know there's a lot going on for me at the moment and I would prefer if she comes the next weekend instead (Action).

- Make a healthy meal for myself after the call (Action).

Step 8: Plan to repair or correct the consequences.
Example: Go for a long walk to ease my stomach. Drink digestive tea to help with digestion. Delay or skip my breakfast the next day to offset some of the effects.

If you often find yourself trapped in the cycle of negative behaviors, BCA is particularly helpful. Now try doing this for one of your problem behaviors.

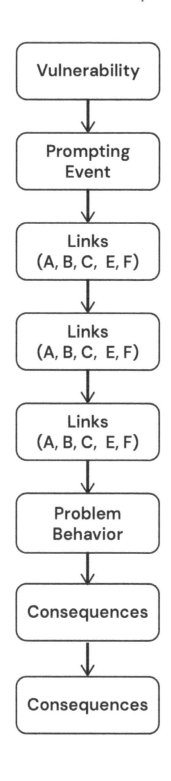

ACTIVITY:
Behavior Chain Analysis

1. Identify the problem behavior.

_____

_____

2. Trace the chain back to get to the prompting event.

_____

_____

_____

_____

3. Examine the links in the chain of events.

- _____

- _____

- _____

- _____

4. Identify vulnerability factors.

_____

_____

_____

_____

5.   Notice the consequences.

Short term -   _____

Long term -   _____

6.   Make a Prevention Plan.

_____

_____

_____

_____

7.   Adopt healthier strategies for each link in the chain.

• _____

• _____

• _____

• _____

TOOL 2:

Mindfulness for Self-Acceptance

Mindfulness helps you to cultivate self-acceptance by non-judgmentally observing your thoughts, feelings, and behaviors. breathing helps you inculcate self-acceptance. When you observe your thoughts without getting caught up in them, it allows you to distance yourself from self-criticism that often comes up. Instead of reacting to a thought or situation, mindfulness enables you to respond. When you observe your thoughts from a curious rather than a judgmental place, you enable yourself to respond differently.

Here are the steps to do it-

- **Mindful Breathing.** Find a calm, quiet place. Close your eyes. Focus on your breath. Notice how your body feels as you breathe in and out. It is okay if your mind wanders. Gently bring your attention back to your breath. Through this activity, you are quieting your endless brain chatter and especially the negative thoughts about the self.

- **Observe your thoughts without judgment.** When thoughts and emotions come up during this practice, let them float by like clouds in the sky. Do not hold onto them. Don't judge yourself based on them. Think of them as temporary and don't let them determine your self-worth.

- **Practice Acceptance.** Remind yourself these are just your thoughts; they are not facts. You do not need to engage with them. Whenever a critical thought comes up, acknowledge it and then bring your focus back to your breath.

- **Reflect.** Once you have completed the exercise, reflect on your experience. How did it feel? Were you able to be non-judgmental? Are there any shifts in your mood?

ACTIVITY:
Mindful Breathing and Observation

Do this activity for 5 minutes right now.

TOOL 3:

Loving-Kindness Meditation

You initiated the process of cultivating self-acceptance in the workbook. Let me teach you loving-kindness meditation to be kinder and more compassionate to yourself and others. This meditation is a mindfulness practice to encourage self-acceptance and inner peace.

Here are the steps to this meditation.

1. Sit comfortably in a calm, quiet place and close your eyes.

2. Imagine yourself in your mind. Silently repeat kind, positive phrases like, "May I be at peace, May I be healthy and happy." Repeat these phrases a few times.

3. Once you feel comfortable, extend these kind wishes to others in your life. Start with close loved ones, then extend these wishes to acquaintances, strangers, and the entire world.

Practicing this meditation reinforces the idea that you and everyone else is worthy of being loved and accepted. It helps you accept yourself for who you are and be kind to others. It helps you develop patience, reduces feelings of stress and anger, and makes you less critical of yourself and others around you. This meditation helps you feel connected to all humanity.

Loving Kindness Meditation

Try to spend 10 minutes meditating using this practice today.

TOOL 4:

Accepting Your Imperfections

Based on our childhood experiences, we are often too critical of ourselves and hold the belief that we need to be perfect to be worthy of love and respect. Using this exercise today, I am encouraging you to embrace your imperfections. You make mistakes as a human and that's normal.

Here are the steps to be followed-

1. Write down your imperfections. What are the things you don't like about yourself or judge yourself about? This could be about your looks, your personality, or certain behavioral aspects.

   Example: 'I am too shy' or 'I am too sensitive.'

2. Reframe these imperfections. Are there any ways in which these imperfections contribute positively to your life?

   Example: 'Because I am shy, I end up finishing up all my work on time as I don't take breaks to socialize or gossip at the office. I have been praised for never missing a deadline.'

   'By being sensitive, I am empathic and mindful of others' emotions that help me connect well with people.'

3. Embrace yourself completely. Reflect on how you can embrace your imperfections along with your strengths.

   Example: "It's okay if I am not perfect. No one is. What matters is that I am learning and growing each day. I accept myself including all my imperfections. They make me human."

ACTIVITY:
Accepting your Imperfections

Now attempt this for yourself.

1. Your imperfections:

   _____

   _____

2. Reframe:

   _____

   _____

3. Reflect and embrace yourself:

   _____

   _____

TOOL 5:

Positive Affirmations

Positive affirmations are positive statements used to challenge a negative mind-set and replace it with constructive and empowered thinking. Example, "I am capable of doing this task," "I deserve to be happy," or "I am lovable." When repeated in a consistent manner, these affirmations hold the power to change the way you think and feel.

Affirmations utilize the concept of neuroplasticity, the ability of our brain to form new connections[19]. When you constantly repeat positive affirmations, you create new pathways in the brain to think and act differently.

A few things to keep in mind while developing positive affirmations:

- They should be personal and specific. Use statements that begin with 'I.' Focus on areas you are struggling with. Example, "I am learning and growing with each passing day."

- Make sure affirmations are in the present sense and not some unknown future time. Instead of saying, "I will stop being anxious soon." Say "I am constantly working on my anxiety."

- Repetition is the key. This is not a one-time magic. If you do not consistently repeat them, they are not going to have an impact. Remember, your negative thoughts have been there for a long time and are resistant to change. Positive affirmations need time to be internalized.

- Include visual reminders. Put them on post-it notes and stick onto your mirror, your notice board, and the wall behind your work desk.

Ideally, try to use them at least once during the time you are facing a mirror. It could be in the morning when you are getting ready. Look yourself in the eye and say them out loud. Do this every day.

ACTIVITY:
Positive Affirmations

Write down three positive affirmations that you resonate with.

1. _____

2. _____

3. _____

4. _____

5. _____

Repeat them now, either out loud or in your mind, over and over again for the next 5 minutes. Visualize what it would feel like to see you embodying these affirmations. Example, if your affirmation is "I am successful," imagine yourself receiving an award from your manager.

References

1 Kasturi, S., Oguoma, V. M., Grant, J. B., Niyonsenga, T., & Mohanty, I. (2023). Prevalence rates of depression and anxiety among young rural and urban Australians: a systematic review and meta-analysis. International journal of environmental research and public health, 20(1), 800.

2 Hofmann, S. G., Asnaani, A., Vonk, I. J., Sawyer, A. T., & Fang, A. (2012). The efficacy of cognitive behavioral therapy: A review of meta-analyses. *Cognitive therapy and research*, 36, 427-440.

3 Lazarus, R. S. (1982). Thoughts on the relations between emotion and cognition. *American psychologist*, 37(9), 1019.

4 National Science Foundation. (n.d.). *National Science Foundation*. Retrieved September 11, 2024, from http://www.nsf.gov/

5 Siyami, M., Moghadam, M. R., & Avaz, K. A. (2023). Investigating the effect of mobile phone use on students' attention span and academic performance. *Journal of Fundamentals of Mental Health*, 25(4).

6 Dizon, R. J., Ermitanio, H. D., Estevez, D. M., Ferrer, J., Flores, S. J., Fontanilla, K. M., ... & Sugay, J. (2021). The effects of pomodoro technique on academic-related tasks, procrastination behavior, and academic motivation among college students in a mixed online learning environment. *Globus Journal of Progressive Education*, 11(2), 58-63.

7 Kennedy, D. R., & Porter, A. L. (2022). The illusion of urgency. *American journal of pharmaceutical education*, 86(7), 8914.

8 Eysenck, M., Payne, S., & Santos, R. (2006). Anxiety and depression: Past, present, and future events. Cognition & Emotion, 20(2), 274-294.

9 Niermann, H. C., Figner, B., & Roelofs, K. (2017). Individual differences in defensive stress-responses: the potential relevance for psychopathology. *Current Opinion in Behavioral Sciences*, 14, 94-101.

10 Guignard, F. P. (2015). Fight, flight, freeze, fool, or pray. Zeitschrift fuer Religionswissenschaft, 23(2), 285.

11 Jerath, R., Crawford, M. W., Barnes, V. A., & Harden, K. (2015). Self-regulation of breathing as a primary treatment for anxiety. *Applied psychophysiology and biofeedback*, 40(2), 107-115.

12 Fumero, A., Peñate, W., Oyanadel, C., & Porter, B. (2020). The effectiveness of mindfulness-based interventions on anxiety disorders. a systematic meta-review. *European Journal of Investigation in Health, Psychology and Education*, 10(3), 704-719.

13 Powers, M. B., & Emmelkamp, P. M. (2008). Virtual reality exposure therapy for anxiety disorders: A meta-analysis. *Journal of anxiety disorders*, 22(3), 561-569.

14 Beck, J. S. (2020). *Cognitive behavior therapy: Basics and beyond.* Guilford Publications.

15 Shaffer, J. (2012). Neuroplasticity and positive psychology in clinical practice: A review for combined benefits. *Psychology*, 3(12), 1110.

16 Stopa, L. (2011). Imagery rescripting across disorders: A practical guide. *Cognitive and Behavioral Practice,* 18(4), 421-423.

17 Norwood, R. (2021). Disrupting Deficit Thinking: Shifting Mindsets One Conversation at a Time (Doctoral dissertation, San Diego State University).

18 American Psychiatric Association. (2015). Depressive disorders: *DSM-5® selections.* American Psychiatric Pub.

19 Tabibnia, G., & Radecki, D. (2018). Resilience training that can change the brain. *Consulting Psychology Journal: Practice and Research,* 70(1), 59.

.